Tropicana **lóqo**

CLOROX

LOGOLO

truvia **lóqo**
Nature's Calorie-Free Sweetener

SAMSUNG

LOGO

Ray-Ban
GENUINE SINCE 1937

Logo-Logo
GENUINE SINCE 1937

skype™

logo™

VISA

D1451915

The Elements of Logo Design
Design Thinking | Branding | Making Marks

Alex W. White

ALLWORTH PRESS
NEW YORK

Cover art Logo interpretations by **Corinne Allyne** *Kellogg's, Samsung* **Brisa Barraza** *ChupaChups, Ford, RayBan, YouTube* **Justin Canas** *ESPN, Goya, Perrier* **Alexia Jandreau** *BurgerKing, Lego, Subway, Visa* **Emmanuel Noi** *Nestlé, Oreo, Tropicana* **Kevin Salmon** *Colgate, Truvía, UGG* **Isaiah Smalls** *Clorox* and **Patrick Zheng** *Skype*

Copyright © 2017 by Alex W. White

All rights reserved. Copyright under Berne Copyright Convention, Universal Copyright Convention, and Pan American Copyright Convention. No part of this book may be reproduced, stored in a retrieval system, or transmitted in any form, or by any means, electronic, mechanical, photocopying, recording or otherwise, without the express written consent of the publisher, except in the case of brief excerpts in critical reviews or articles. All inquiries should be addressed to Allworth Press, 307 West 36th Street, 11th Floor, New York, NY 10018.

Allworth Press books may be purchased in bulk at special discounts for sales promotion, corporate gifts, fund-raising, or educational purposes. Special editions can also be created to specifications. For details, contact the Special Sales Department, Allworth Press, 307 West 36th Street, 11th Floor, New York, NY 10018 or info@skyhorsepublishing.com.

22 21 20 19 18   5 4 3 2 1

Published by Allworth Press, an imprint of Skyhorse Publishing, Inc. 307 West 36th Street, 11th Floor, New York, NY 10018.

Allworth Press® is a registered trademark of Skyhorse Publishing, Inc.®, a Delaware corporation.

www.allworth.com

Cover and interior design by Alex W. White

Library of Congress Cataloging-in-Publication Data

Names: White, Alex (Alex W.), author.
Title: The elements of logo design : design thinking | branding | making marks / Alex W. White.
Description: New York, New York : Allworth Press, An imprint of Skyhorse Publishing, Inc., 2018. | Includes index.
Identifiers: LCCN 2018015576 (print) | LCCN 2018016061 (ebook) | ISBN 9781621536031 (eBook) | ISBN 9781621536741 (pbk. : alk. paper)
Subjects: LCSH: Logos (Symbols)--Design.
Classification: LCC NC1002.L63 (ebook) | LCC NC1002.L63 W53 2018 (print) |
    DDC 741.6--dc23
LC record available at https://lccn.loc.gov/2018015576

Hardcover ISBN: 978-1-62153-602-4
Paperback ISBN: 978-1-62153-674-1
Ebook ISBN: 978-1-62153-603-1

Printed in China

FOREWORD When I think back to studying graphic design in the 1970s at the University of Cincinnati and later for four years at the Basel School of Design, I don't recall ever seeing a book on the process of logo design. There were books full of logo examples, but my passion for logos came from the student–teacher model of working on assignments and learning from individual and group critiques.

Today it has never been easier to design logos. There is wide appreciation and demand for logos from companies and organizations. Programs such as Adobe Illustrator have facilitated the creative process and enabled designers to explore possibilities that were far more laborious in the past. But today is also a particularly challenging period for logo design. The same tools that help designers also make it easier for others to create a multitude of less effective solutions. Styles spread much faster than knowledge.

Pre-Internet, it might have taken years before work designed, for example in Japan, would be seen abroad. Now we can see it immediately.

While there have been tremendous changes in all aspects of logo design, the core qualities of an effective logo have not changed. *Strong*, *distinct*, *memorable*, *flexible*, and *enduring* are the same fundamental attributes I still strive to achieve after three decades. *Enduring* is perhaps the most difficult to achieve. Whether for a small start-up or a major company, the goal is not to appear trendy or it will likely look dated in the future. A stinging (and usually inaccurate) comment on logo review sites is often a version of "The eighties want their logo back."

One of the best ways to avoid being trendy is to be knowledgeable about the history of logo design. A particularly revealing example is the design of the Olympic games

AT&T, after its breakup in 1982, required a name and logo without any reference to the Bell name and icon. Our team at Saul Bass generated over 2,000 logos for the initial exploration leading to the global telecommunications symbol. *Designer: Jerry Kuyper, Firm: Saul Bass, Herb Yager & Associates 1983.*

Cisco Systems, founded in 1984, used an abstraction of the Golden Gate Bridge as its logo. By 2005 the company was on its fourth bridge logo and still not satisfied. John Chambers specified he wanted to see some DNA of the bridge in our work. *Designer: Jerry Kuyper and Joe Finocchiaro, Firm: Jerry Kuyper Partners 2006*

logos from 1948–2016 (*see page 84*). The transition from the detailed Romulus, Remus, and wolf for Rome 1960 to the simple red circle for Japan 1964 is a major stride forward. The Olympic logos don't need to last decades, just the four-year period leading up to the games. By comparison, most companies would like their logos to last for decades. Former General Electric CEO Jack Welch, referring to GE's rebranding in 1986, is purported to have said, "GE hasn't taken a serious look at their visual identity in seventy-five years. We want to make sure we get it right because we don't want to have to revisit it for *another* seventy-five years."

Before starting Jerry Kuyper Partners in 2004, I spent twenty years working with Saul Bass, Walter Landor, Siegel & Gale, and Lippincott. While at Saul Bass in the early 1980s, I was the lead designer on the original AT&T globe. It has undergone at least three significant updates in the last thirty-plus years.

In a review of the most recent change, it was suggested that the original mark is still the most effective. Another comment was that the original 1984 version anticipated the recent trend toward flat design. Our goal in 1984 was to make the globe look as dimensional as possible, but with an economy of means: using no glows, gradations, or shadows. Simple concepts expressed clearly tend to last longer than embellishment techniques.

This book stands out because it discusses graphic design principles and then shows how they apply to logo design. It has fresh insights and different thinking on the process of logo design. I am delighted to welcome Alex's thoughtful book to my library.

Jerry Kuyper
Westport, CT

WWF had been using two different pandas, one for the US and one for the rest of the world. They realized the need for a single global symbol. We examined the existing marks but went back to the source, the panda, for inspiration. *Design director: Jerry Kuyper, Designer: Jenny Leibundgut, Firm: Landor 1987*

Cigna wanted its logo to retain the visual heritage of its Tree of Life, focus on the importance of the individual, suggest the company's global presence, and convey a healthy optimism. The colors are direct neighbors — two primaries and a secondary — on the color wheel. *Designer: Jerry Kuyper, Firm: Jerry Kuyper Partners 2011*

INTRODUCTION This book is for designers. Except *these two pages*. These two pages are very special: these pages are for *clients*. Of course, designers skip them at their own peril.

Dear businessperson who is planning a new logo: if you accept that logos are a significant component to brand building, and brands should not be invisible, and making something visible requires taking a risk to stand out, then please consider the following points. Many of the samples in this book are for very small companies who actually want and, because of their size, *need* to make a killer impression — and are emotionally equipped to take a risk in the way they represent their businesses.

Businesspeople dress for meetings in clothes that are neat and presentable but not too edgy or noticeable. What kind of businesspeople go to a meeting *not* wearing tasteful though safe Brooks Brothers? *Hungry nonconformists who revel in being — and appearing — different.*

Creating cool design is much harder than merely giving clients what they ask for. It takes vision and creativity to turn an obvious set of criteria (what most clients provide) into a fresh, memorable, "creative" expression of the real, underlying problem. The given problem, the assignment you give your well-paid consultants, must be turned inside out. Not all designers are equipped to do it. But you have to give your designers a *chance* to excel, else you will surely end up with mediocrity.

Design is the marriage of *need* and *useful expression*. Apple is the coolest industrial design right now, having given Sony, the previous leader, a spanking, because of Apple's strict adherence to making tools work the way they *should*, not the way they always *have*. It takes vision from the client — and clear vision from designers — to achieve excellence like that. Most clients start out wanting fresh, innovative, and noticeable design, then dilute

"Design" cannot be bought from a catalog. It isn't a widget or a product. Design is a human visual vocabulary that is a parallel language with as many subtleties and shadings and nuanced meanings as the verbal one. Unfortunately, design doesn't have a dictionary or thesaurus. It is all custom-crafted. Choose a designer who understands that and trust his or her educated and experienced explanation.

Do you expect there to be a measurable result for the investment you are making in your logo? Unfortunately, design doesn't work that way. The visual impression you make is *one part* of an overall experience of your company or product. To expect more than that is to reveal a lack of understanding of visual quality. Businesspeople typically give in reluctantly when they are persuaded to invest in the necessary work, then are shown it, *and* when the difference between quality and dross is explained to them. Even then they remain unconvinced until the bottom line shows some kind of upward motion (which they attribute to something else, of course). To them, "design" is surface decoration to make it look cool.

it during multiple group meetings, until the result is common, expected, and frustrating for everyone at the table. You think, "If I'd hired a *good* designer, I'd have gotten better work." They think, "If this sh*t-for-brains had left well enough alone, the message delivery and design would have been outstanding, but it got familiarized down to typical mediocre crap."

Here's an exercise to do with your management team: pick a magazine and pull out all the ads, then arrange them in order of "most visible" to "most banal." Where is the demarcation between "pretty good" and "ordinary"? About 10–20 percent in from the end. Why do the other 80–90 percent stink — and by "stink," I mean they are *invisible*? Is it the bad choice of an ad agency? Much more likely, it is the misguided involvement of too many people, which ends up making a message *less* visible, *less* potent, and *less* useful. Hire the best, challenge them to do their best, and don't get in their way.

As a businessperson, what do you imagine is the working process that leads to design samples that *you* think are interesting and fun? How much do you think the client imposed his or her opinion and (lack of) design talent on the designer? As a businessperson, do you think:

☐ there is likely to be *or*

☐ there is *not* likely to be

a correlation between uninformed client opinions and mediocre design?

The very best thing to do as the client is prepare a comprehensive project brief that includes measurable goals (so you will accept the results even if the design "looks risky"), then hire the best designer and challenge him so he will deliver a unique and unknowable solution to your well-stated problem.

Alex W. White

Greenwich, CT

If you're going to get a dog, you really ought to let the dog do your barking. Innovative design, like innovative business thinking, results when the best are hired and challenged to outdo themselves. Ordinary design, like ordinary business thinking, results when you hire good people and tie their hands with uninformed opinions. As the client, please think very carefully before making changes to a design. Yes, you have the authority to make changes, but that doesn't mean your changes will be in the best interest of the project. As a businessperson, if you could really design, you'd save money by not hiring a designer at all and doing "great" creative thinking yourself. Don't dilute the power of design, which is necessary to *the needs of your targets*.

Watch out if your designer gives you a collection of visual clichés that appear to be a "choice." This is not responsible professional practice because it is based on what she likes, not solutions to your specific problem. Such work is totally surface. Pretense. Decorating. This is not true advice, which actually should cost you an arm and a leg. It is opinion and taste, which certainly has its place, but not as the dominant attribute of your new logo.

Having "nothing wrong" with a design is a long way from having "something right" with it. If you can state what is *right* with your work, you have applied logical thought. If not, random prevails.

If it's random it's wrong.

**Five Steps
to Improve
Using Logic
Your Design
to Refine
Process
a Design Idea**

Chapter 1

Design is often thought of as an artistic, intuitive activity, but it isn't really that at all. At least few *targets* think of it that way.

Design is actually a service that is supposed to give messages stopping power and make their meaning and value plain. Done right, design adds value and is well worth every dollar paid to the designer.

On the other hand, design as decoration or mere layout is a distraction and rarely worth the investment by a client. Worse, it isn't effective on a target's awareness. When properly applied, design is a tool that engages the viewer and pushes a message forward.

As designers, we are "thought manipulators" and collectively, we have trained our targets to ignore our messages out of their own self-preservation. It doesn't matter what kind of design you do: your targets are attacked by 4,500 advertising (sales) and editorial (information) messages per day.

It is as if our audience has mosquito netting over their heads and your message is an irritating mosquito. How do we get our messages through our targets' nearly mosquito-proof netting? ※ *Every* message has to fight its way into a target's awareness. There are simply too many of them being thrown at us every day.

So what gets your message noticed and gets targets to give it the attention you want for it? Give visual messages stopping power — make them noticed — by daring to make them sufficiently different from their surroundings.

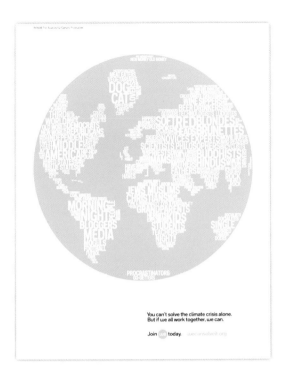

That means making messages a bit abstract and, perhaps counterintuitively, *reducing* their legibility. Keep in mind, however, that all sacrifices to increase visibility have to be in service to the message's real meaning.

Relationships
Contrast and Similarity
Hierarchy
Structure
Color

We'll look at five ways to use logic to develop appropriate abstraction and increase a message's visibility. These may be absorbed subconsciously by your readers, but your work will be enhanced by intentionally attending to them.

STEP 1 Relationships

Think of "design" as a verb — an action word, not as a noun — a thing. Design is a *process*, not a *result*. The purpose of the process is to develop more meaningful solutions and more apparent relationships among the visible elements of the design. The best solution evolves through iterations, through a sequence of studies each leading to additional possibilities.

The design process is one of refining *intentional relationships between parts*. The clearer the relationships, the better the design. Another way of saying this is a design that lacks relationships is just a group of unrelated parts, which is essentially where elements begin their journey without a designer's intervention.

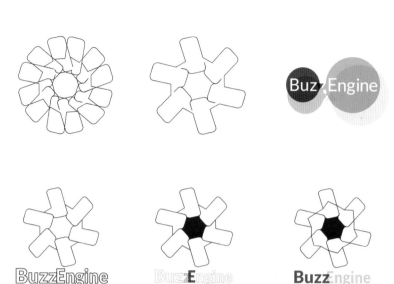

Lato Hairline *Lato Hairline Italic*
Lato Light *Lato Light Italic*
Lato Regular *Lato Italic*
Lato Bold ***Lato Bold Italic***
Lato Black ***Lato Black Italic***

Aaᵃ ÁáÀàÂâÅåÄäÃãĄąÆ
æB bCcĆćÇçDdÐ ðEeÉéÈ
èÊêËëĘęFfﬁﬂſGg Hh IiÍíÌì
ÎîÏïJjKkLlŁł ɫMm Nn Ńń Ññ
O o °ÓóÒòÔôÖöÕõØøŒ
œPpQq RrSsŚśŠšßTt ™Uu
ÚúÙùÛûÜü VvWwXxYy
Ýý Ÿÿ ZzŹźŽžŻż Þþ 01 ¹ ½ ¼

These studies show alternative marks for an events management and brand activation company. The Lato type family, an open-source typeface by Polish designer Łukasz Dziedzic, was required. The designers were asked explicitly to avoid bees and train engines, as neither has anything to do with the company. Besides, merely illustrating nouns is a too-easy solution that doesn't show insight or add value to a message.

Lettermarks

Wordmarks

Pictorial Marks

Abstract Marks

Combination Marks

The designers were each asked to develop a series of fifteen studies, producing three different lettermarks, wordmarks, pictorial marks, abstract marks, and combination marks. This process causes a breadth of ideas to evolve.

As stated earlier, design is the result of conscious relationship building between unrelated parts. Indeed, the quality of a design is determined by the quality and clarity of the relationships that unify or fail to unify the parts.

Studies almost always begin with an emphasis on the figure — the image and letterforms — and gradually shift over to balancing the figures with the space behind, bringing space forward.

The company's tagline — "We get people talking" — was added to studies to show how it would be integrated with and enhance the existing relationships rather than look like a pasted-on outlier.

The designers each chose their two best marks and optimized them to grayscale and bitmap (black and white) modes. This is not necessarily as easy as simply choosing image translations on the computer: adjustments have to be made so each iteration looks equivalently intentional.

STEP 2 Contrast and Similarity

Contrast and similarity are opposite sides of a single idea: one obliges the other. Contrast makes design visible. Similarity — lack of contrast — makes design look like a bowl of oatmeal: an eventless monotone of gray. Figure/ground is the strongest inherent contrast. These marks craft ground so it becomes the foreground figure.

Complete similarity — single line thickness of the name "Green Tea" — compares with complete contrast in a mark for a massage therapist, which uses a stone rubbing of an at-rest *R* to reference ancient Italian spas. Design can begin with a complete lack of harmony (too much contrast) and move toward greater harmony, or begin with complete harmony (too much similarity) and add only as much contrast as necessary.

ROMAN

Creation and hard work

 Bio-science

 Primary natural resource

 Healthy and sparkling with energy

 Paradise

 Fresh ingredients

 Sustainability

 Pleasure and enjoyment

 Freedom

Purity

 Fresh laundry

 Love, care, and health

 Sensitivity and fragrance

 Blending flavors

 Delicious-smelling foods

 Packaging

 Beauty and taste

 Nutrition

 Looking good

 Freshness

 Sea and fresh water

Science

 Cleanliness

 Growing

Contrasting symbols — each with their own meaning — are unified by size and equal spacing in this international conglomerate's redesigned mark. No matter how you begin a design, there comes a time when squeezing out every bit of *unnecessary* contrast is the right move. Think of your design as a soapy sponge that needs to run clean. The sponge takes repeated rinsings — one or two more contrasts that can be tamed.

Contrast studies begin with a collection of foreign samples (*top left*). The meaning of the words is not important in contrast studies: the *form* of the letters and words is. Five limitations are placed on the use of these elements: typeface use, alignments, letterspacing, line spacing, and baseline agreement. These limitations, which *cause* creativity, are explored in both organic and grid-based design, producing at least ten studies.

STEP 3 Hierarchy

Hierarchy lends order to our perception of the elements. Order defined by comparative importance is a road map for readers, guiding them through the parts of a design. Hierarchy is essential to make the most important element stand out and to show descending importance. Developing hierarchy is less about making one thing stand out (size and weight contrast are typically used to reveal a headline, for example) as it is making everything but the focal point *the same*. ❀ At top is the required content of this exercise, from which one complete set must be used. The exercise explores the balance between abstract word forms and their meaning: how much abstraction is too much? This sheet of typeset copy is certainly legible, but it isn't designed to reveal importance or meaning. ❀ Each study must express one of five design principles: unification vs. isolation; direction; rhythm; texture and value; and spatial depth.

Provided content

Unification/Isolation

Direction

Rhythm

Texture and Value

Spatial Depth

Each study *must emphasize a different part of the message.* Because design is a problem-solving *process*, creativity is supported by giving limitations. Infinite freedom — for example by saying "make a design" — leads to discussions about what everybody likes instead of solving real problems. Design thinking requires solving real problems, even abstract real problems. Exploring problem-solving techniques is central to the mission of design learning.

Unification/Isolation

Hierarchy is essential to make the most important element stand out and to show relative importance. Three levels of hierarchy is the ideal: readers recognize most important, least important, and all the rest in the middle. These studies express *unification vs. isolation*, so a focal point is made to stand out of unified secondary and tertiary information. These studies also need to consider relative position to create their anomaly and focal point.

Direction contrast is used on these four studies to reveal the focal point. It is very difficult to have only one contrast at a time, so weight and color are also used in some of these studies to indicate hierarchy.

Direction

Rhythm requires elements to appear in regular positions and the element that breaks that regularity is seen as the focal point. The development of a *system* is essential to the success of these studies so the anomaly can be seen.

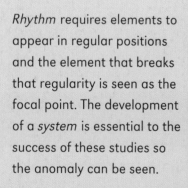
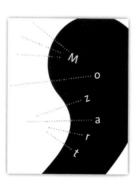

Rhythm

Texture/Value

Texture is ordinarily a surface description. The rougher the surface, the better it translates into two-dimensional imagery. But texture is also a term used to describe areas of type. *Value* is simply the lightness or darkness of an area. These studies use either or both terms to create a system from which the focal point is revealed.

Spatial Depth

Spatial depth studies suggest the third dimension in two-dimensional studies. The first two dimensions are height and width. The system can be either two dimensional or three dimensional, and the focal point contrasts the system.

STEP 4 Structure

Structure is the underlying anatomy of the elements, the invisible bones of a composition. There are two kinds of structure: internal structure and external structure. These examples are of internal structure: the placement of parts is dependent on the elements. At top, two marks using the shapes of the letters *UCDA* and *NUDE* produce comparable results. Beneath is an ad for a watch that strikingly lacks an hour hand.

Both internal and external structures make unrelated elements look like they belong together for design unity: a singular impression made from many parts. ❋ External structure is imposed on the elements by fitting them on a grid, which limits sizes and positions. The top row shows the required 25-unit grid, the imagery (Christo and Jeanne-Claude's *The Gates*), and the required type (Portuguese song lyrics).

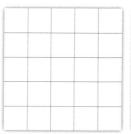

M'pensá na nha vida mi sô
Sem ninguem di fé, perto di mim
Pa st'ojdá qués ondas ta 'squebrá di mansinho
Ta trazé-me um dor di sentimento

M'pensá

na nha vida mi sô Sem ninguem di fé, perto di mim

Pa st'ojdá qués ondas ta 'squebrá di mansinho Ta trazé-me um dor di sentimento

M'pensá

na nha vida mi sô Sem ninguem di fé, perto di mim

Pa st'ojdá qués ondas ta 'squebrá di mansinho Ta trazé-me um dor di sentimento

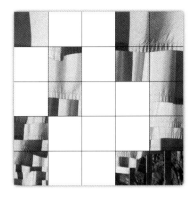
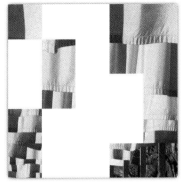

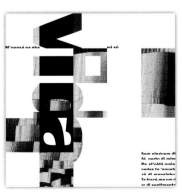

This exercise explores ways image, type, and space can interact into a single impression. Abstraction is enthusiastically encouraged. ❈ A grid is best used to chop away or "cover over" bits of the imagery and letterforms placed on it. This causes the ground to be seen as figure. The top row shows the grid over the image and the resulting image and space study. The second row shows type and space studies, and the bottom two rows show type, image, and space studies. The process imposed on the designer causes such abstraction, which in turn allows hierarchy to be developed and revealed. ❈ The final studies are refined, sophisticated sets of design relationships that draw attention and communicate meaningfully. Note the process that brought the simple raw material on the facing page to life.

STEP 5 Color

Color is a raw material to be used strategically for a clear purpose. It is a tool that can be used to either relate or differentiate. Color and shape are the most important parts of a logo, but color use in general has the same potential for communicating hierarchy as typeface, weight, size, or placement contrasts. Color can be used to direct and guide, or its random application will work against clarity and understanding, just as do any other random design changes. 🎴 Color adds interest, as in these variations on playing cards. It can be used as part of an identity program over repeat exposures to say a company has flexibility and a certain "break the rules" philosophy. And color is often used as a central part of a visual branding strategy, as this bank's billboard illustrates.

THAT'S HOW IT IS

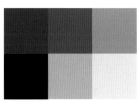

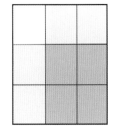

MPEG 4

QED-GlobalCycle.m4a

A limiting selection of type-faces and paragraph styles and spacing between elements is common practice. Using a limited color palette — a pre-selected set of colors — ensures color unity and design consistency over time and messages. ❦ Define what's most useful and valuable to your reader by giving color to emphasize that part. Plan color use from the start. If color is added at the end, it is likely to only be a surface cosmetic.

Identity design requires dis-tinctive colors for recognition in the marketplace. These decisions have to be made in the context of direct competitors' colors as well as generalized use of the colors you may be considering.

The color wheel shows the relationships of colors, or *hues*. *Value* is the lightness or darkness of a hue, as shown in *tints*, the addition of white, and *shades*, the addition of black. *Saturation* (or *chroma* or *intensity*) is the brightness or dullness of a hue. *Primary colors* are red, blue, and yellow. Secondary colors are orange, green, and purple, because they are combinations of primary colors. Tertiary colors are yellow-orange, yellow-green, etc.

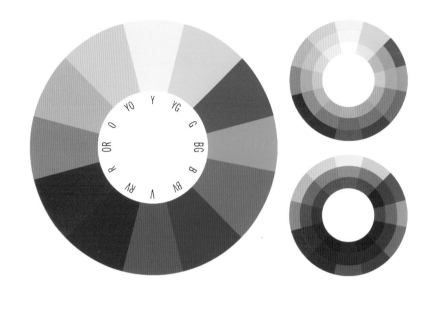

Complementary colors are opposite each other on the color wheel and naturally look good together. *Analogous colors* are next to each other on the color wheel. *Triadic harmonies* are three colors equally spaced on the color wheel.

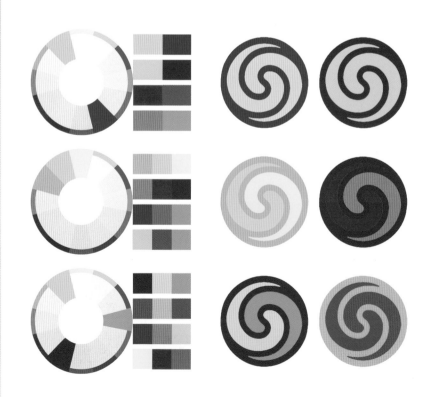

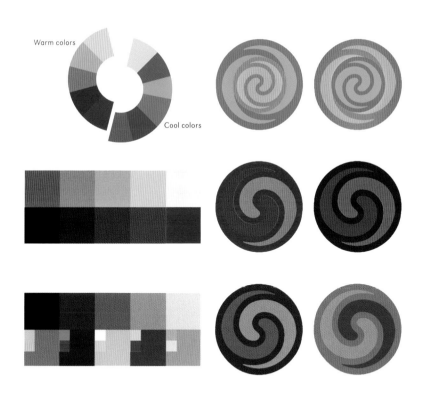

Warm colors appear closer and *cool colors* appear farther away. *Monochromatic colors* are a single hue with their tints and shades. *Achromatic colors* are shades of black or the neutral grays made by mixing complementary colors.

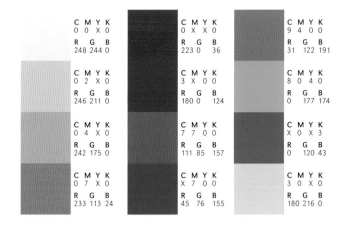

C M Y K	C M Y K	C M Y K
0 0 X 0	0 X X 0	9 4 0 0
R G B	R G B	R G B
248 244 0	223 0 36	31 122 191
C M Y K	C M Y K	C M Y K
0 2 X 0	3 X 0 0	8 0 4 0
R G B	R G B	R G B
246 211 0	180 0 124	0 177 174
C M Y K	C M Y K	C M Y K
0 4 X 0	7 7 0 0	X 0 X 3
R G B	R G B	R G B
242 175 0	111 85 157	0 120 43
C M Y K	C M Y K	C M Y K
0 7 X 0	X 7 0 0	3 0 X 0
R G B	R G B	R G B
233 113 24	45 76 155	180 216 0

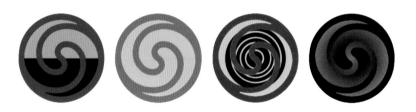

RGB (Red Blue Green) is the designation for on-screen color and for local printing. *CMYK* (Cyan Magenta Yellow Black) is the designation for colors in preparation for four-color printing. CMYK files are 25 percent bigger than RGB files because they have a quarter more data, so CMYK should be used only when four-color printing is the intended result. Shown here are color formula equivalencies. In CMYK parlance, "X" means 100 percent.

The definition of design is *to plan*. A plan is revealed by making things look like they are supposed to be *precisely that way*. Creating relationships results in *design unity*, the goal of all design.

Design excellence
is defined by
the quality of the
relationships
you create:
no relationships,
no design.

Chapter 2

Forcing elements to relate makes a design powerful. Placing the headline (or "primary type") into the image unifies the parts of this design into a single visual statement.

Art challenges. Art provokes. Art enlightens. Above all, art is a catalyst that helps people embrace new perspectives. Just as art expands the world of possibilities, we share fresh perspectives with our clients to help create tailored investment solutions. It's a relationship we call "You & Us."

UBS is the proud main sponsor of Art Basel and Art Basel Miami Beach.

Art | Basel | Miami Beach

Wealth Management | Global Asset Management | Investment Bank   You & Us   ✷ UBS

Adding design to a raw, undesigned message — passing a message through a designer's mind — is supposed to do two things: make the message noticeable, and make its value immediately evident. A mechanical process like this grid can produce unexpected results that describe the intended idea clearly.

London   Short-Order Cooks   London Short-Order Cooks

There is *better* design and there is *worse* design. The determining factor is not the parts being used, it is the *quality of the relationships* among the parts. Designers use just three elements: type, image, and space. In terms of visual form, these elements almost never have anything in common in the beginning of the design process.

So good design is a matter of balancing contrasts and similarities — opposing conditions — among unlike parts. ❦ *This* is design unity, where each part shares some attributes with the others but retains a degree of *meaningful* contrast to provide visual energy.

Without *similarity*, it isn't possible to create an environment of quietness that gives an important element the opportunity to be seen. ❀ Without *contrast*, a design will be uneventful, gray, and dull and will almost certainly fail to be noticed, the very first job of every visual message. The copy in gray on this business card aligns with the gray pills, making the one red pill stand out as a focal point.

PharmDr. Anna Hudlerová
Za Skalkou 778/11, 147 00 Praha 4
+420 739 442 211 ahudler@pharm.cz

William A. Dwiggins was memorably quoted as having said, *"Unity contributes orderliness and coherency and a civilized state of things generally. Whereas the contrast family are all savages, more or less."* Design is largely about balancing similarity (gold color and organic strokes) and contrast (geometric circle and straight rays) to make a tasty whole.

A unified design is considerably more visible and potent than it's alternative: a mere assembly of random pieces that have nothing in common. This brewery branding system allows for variation within a strict color, type, and symbol palette.

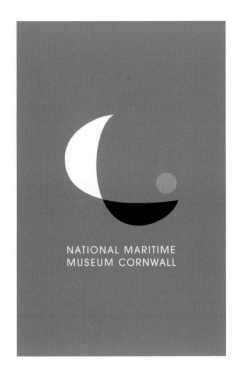

Unity is the value we designers add, and we'll look at two areas in which unity can be developed: *contrast*, the natural state of things, the "before," and *similarity*, the designer's "after" and the application of external design requirements on all elements to *force* unity on them equally.

Differences and Consistencies

When you are setting out to make a design, what exactly are you preparing to do? Make some stuff æsthetically attractive? Make it handsome? Make it "look good"? Loose drawing in a cartoon style certainly achieves those objectives, as in this mark for a comic about a group of Spanish tapas living as illegal immigrants in Queens, New York.

You're probably starting with some type (or thoughts described in words), some imagery (or thoughts described visually), and an empty field (as background, a page, or screen). How you relate them is all important.

Lucidiai Media LLC

The first problem is choosing which pieces to use. Type decisions include overall character or personality, content, typeface, size, weight, caps or lowercase, color, and position.

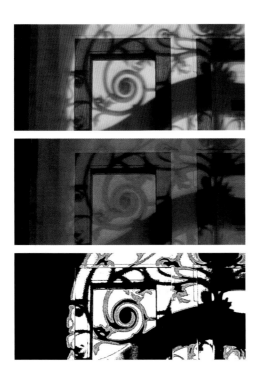

Image decisions include content, photo or illustration, color or grayscale or black and white, cropping, size, and position. ❀ Space decisions include how much of it to fill in, whether to impose space on the type and imagery through the use of a grid, and, if using a grid, whether to bring some of it to the foreground.

After you've considered the use of the three elements — type, image, and space — the second problem is that these pieces don't have much in common.

They have differences by the bucketful. Type is fundamentally different than image: it takes effort to read, it must be arranged in sequence to make sense, and it must be reasonably clear to read to fulfill its purpose as an information delivery system. Make type and image relate: here they share color, drawing quality, and shape. The further you can get from a typeset mark, the more distinctive, as here for a San Francisco foodie club.

A NEW WAY TO HOTEL

AC
HOTELS
MARRIOTT
AC-HOTELS.COM

Image is an easier way to convey meaning and takes less work to absorb, but image is more open to misunderstanding. That is why a caption, whether as small type or a headline, is usually placed nearby — to explain the intended meaning. "A NEW WAY TO HOTEL" and the AC HOTEL logo are instrumental in making the imagery clear in this ad.

And space, well, space is the antithesis of the other two elements. It is the *absence* of content. So it is very tricky to make it behave like either type or image. Here, space is manipulated through layering abstracted Viking helmets into the crowded letterforms, one echoing in its pattern the siding on a new campus building. Design unity requires that type, image, and space share attributes, that they have similarities. Design is no more complicated than that.

The default design relationship is *proximity*: "these things are related because they are simply near each other." They don't need to share any other design attributes.

What defines good and great design from average, adequate, or mediocre design is the quality of the relationships — the unity — among the parts, *not* the parts themselves. ❧ It really doesn't matter much *to the reader* if you choose Myriad or Gotham — because they are so *similar*.

Myriad   Gotham

Both set in Myriad

Myriad   Gotham

Both set in Gotham

Myriad   Preissig

Both set in Myriad

Myriad   Preissig

Both set in Preissig

It matters much more if you choose Myriad or, say, Preissig because they are so *different*. ❋ It matters a great deal to the browser that the type has something in common with the imagery, that its choice and use is purposeful, not random.

Interestingly, image choice and use is never random: the meaning and composition of the image is understood to be paramount. Why should type choice and use receive any less consideration?

"REALLY, OLD BOY, YOU AREN'T SUPPOSED TO BUILD THAT SORT OF THING IN AMERICA, Y'KNOW."

CORVETTE *by Chevrolet*

DON'T FEAR THE MEATBALL. Soft and strong like cloth. Viva towels. Think big little.

Viva

The starting point in design is stuff that doesn't relate except, probably, in meaning. And our job is to make them visually relate to give the totality design unity so the message gains visibility and potency. Here the background pattern has been brought into the type, and architectural details have been brought into the pattern.

How to Create Similarity and Unity
Shared size
Playing with scale so everything is one weight or size is a terrific way to achieve similarity. This is the artwork for a tattoo in Latin that reads *"vox audita perit litera scripta manet"* which translates to "The spoken word perishes but the written word remains."

MUSEUM OF BOULDER

Shared color

Pulling a color out of an image — an *important* color from the *subject* rather than just any color from any part of the image — is a standard treatment for creating similarity between type and image.

Shared shape

Everything shaped with a definite soft roundness, for example, has similarity. The image and letterforms in this example look like they were autotraced.

Shared position (proximity)
The simplest way to achieve similarity is to place elements close together. This is a mark for a specialized sports health website. Note the subtle golf-ball-on-the-edge-of-the-cup reference.

Alignment
Elements that line up appear related. The invisible horizontal line that runs through the midpoint of the red square unites the DZ characters below it and the GROUP above it.

ERG
ENERGY CO.

Shared texture

Any visual attribute will work to join elements: texture, pattern, edge treatment, a weird material, etc. The more distinctive, the better.

Repetition

Repeat elements' position to create rhythm and unity. Flipping and rotating elements ensures design unity and certain symmetry, as in this temporary tattoo design by an American type foundry.

A drawback with technology is that the choice of elements one can use is infinite, or very nearly so. ❦ In the absence of limitations, random choices are inevitable — and when you combine unlimited choice with no particular idea, a weak or merely adequate design is the result.

So give yourself external limitations, a narrowing of choices that causes you to make visible relationships. Here are some examples of creating design unity with assigned pieces: a typeface (an authorized free download directly from the font's designer) and randomly selected words and image from the Internet. Working with elements that have nothing to do with each other makes "right design thinking" clearly evident when it happens.

Yanone Kaffeesatz Bold

european parliament elections

be what one is

Required typeface
Yanone Kaffeesatz Bold

Required primary type
Wikipedia Random Article
headline

Required secondary type
Quotationspage
last four words

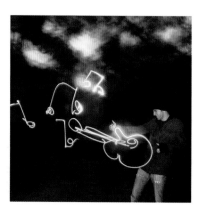

Required image
Flickr Interesting Photos

Symmetrical balance with rules

SYMMETRY: Visually equal on both sides. Symmetry does not require a mirror image. The sides may be *reasonably equivalent*. Asymmetry ("Not symmetry," or "Not the same on both sides") doesn't become apparent until symmetry is significantly adjusted. // **RULE: A line.** Not necessarily a straight, computer-drawn line.

Assigning exercises like this *causes* design relationships to be created and encourages experimental, exploratory work that absolutely would not happen otherwise. **Symmetrical balance with rules** puts space into the background, where it is typically submissive to both type and image: it is seen around and behind elements and only very rarely is space in the *foreground* — forcing itself into a dominant position over the figures in it.

²/₃ type dominance

DOMINANCE: To take precedence over; superior or commanding. Dominance can be made visible two ways: simply, by comparative size or area covered; or more difficultly, by forcing the dominated element to bend to the requirements of the dominating element. Space is typically forced to be submissive to both type and image placed in it, that is, space is seen around and behind elements and only very rarely is it in the foreground — forcing itself into a dominant position over figures in it.

Two-thirds type dominance
An imbalance for a dynamic design between type and image must be pronounced to be noticeable. Two-thirds or three-quarters dominance are necessary. Managing the elements for the precise balance of two-thirds dominance is a powerful way to focus designers' attention and help them achieve intentionality and control of their designs.

Another way of forcing a relationship is **bleeding image on three sides**. Bleeding is printing imagery or type to trim. Bleeding implies continuation beyond the edge, so this study actually explores infinite and finite space. ❊ These studies must *have* the image bleed on three of those edges and must *use* image nonbleed on the fourth edge. So this design asks the question "How can I *use* any design attribute effectively?"

A fourth way of forcing a relationship is **shared transparency**. In this case, "share" means "common," and transparency means "allowing light to pass through so what is beneath can be seen."

Image bleeds three sides

BLEED: Printing imagery or type to trim. To avoid a sliver of unprinted paper from showing if trimming is off register, design elements that are to bleed must extend beyond trim by 1 pica. The four edges of a framal reference are head, foot, left, and right.

Shared transparency

SHARE: A part or portion that is divided between two or more, portion out, allocate; possess in common with others. TRANSPARENCY: Allowing light to pass through so what is beneath can be seen.

Transparent elements reveal relationships by "ultimate overlapping." It is the pinnacle of relating by proximity or nearness: the elements occupy the exact same space.

Shared texture with rules

SHARE: A part or portion that is divided between two or more, portion out, allocate; possess in common with others. TEXTURE: The tactile feel or consistency of a surface; touch. RULE: A line, though not necessarily a straight, computer-generated line.

And the final way I asked my students to craft relationships is through **shared texture with rules**. Again, "share" means "common"; a texture is the tactile feel or consistency of a surface (a texture is not a pattern, which is purely visual, not touchable); and a rule is a line, though not necessarily a computer-generated geometric line.

These five ways of forcing relationships are arbitrary but serve to focus thinking and creativity. While there are nearly an infinite number of ways of forcing a relationship among elements, they all share the purpose of defining a more specific problem to solve and applying a treatment to all elements similarly so *the elements look like they belong together.*

Unity is a condition in which all the parts of a design are coaxed into working together to make a single, powerful, *value-added* impression on the viewer. Unity comes from forcing *similarity* on dissimilar parts of type, image, and space. Applying an outside idea or a design treatment to all elements are effective ways of achieving design unity.

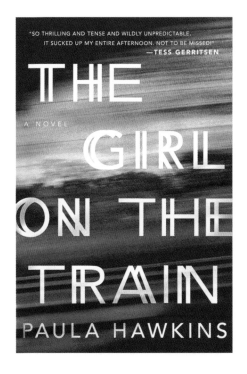

The quality of a design is determined by the quality of the *relationships* between the type, image, and space, not on the quality of the individual parts themselves. ❊ Design unity is the result of making choices that are consciously "right" so that parts grow in similarity and are not just individually "nice" or "attractive."

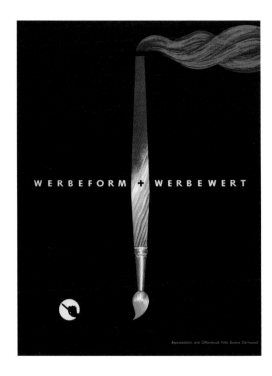

The difference between a "thing" (a nondesign made with random choices and relationships) and a *right-thinking* design made with precise relationships is design *unity*. This geometrically balanced 1951 full-page ad for a German printer says "Advertising Form + Advertising Effect" and shows a combination of art and industry.

Typography has rules that evolved over centuries and which can be quickly found on the Internet. Thoughtfully breaking rules can make type *look right*, and type that looks right *is right*.

Maybe

The simplest definition of art is a true lie.

3
53

"If you celebrate it, it's art. If you don't, it isn't." John Cage, Composer

Chapter 3

You have a message. If you speak it, it is to be *heard*. If you write it, it is to be *read*. Spoken and written language have been unified — marks correlate to specific sounds — since the Phœnicians developed the idea in about 1200 BC.

Letterforms, which are abstract symbols, can be said to be "frozen sound," because the marks represent *phonemes*, the smallest parts of spoken language. Phonemes are either vowels (a, e, i, o, u) or consonants. Typography is therefore "frozen speech." What foreign language is being described with these image symbols?

How to do things right

How to do things right?

How to do things right?

How to do things right?

Porsche + Geese = "Portuguese"

A speaker uses emphases and changes in rhythm and volume to enliven his delivery and hold his audience's interest. Just so with good typography. Visual language requires emphases, pauses, and changes in rhythm and volume to hold a reader's attention. Reading aloud helps a designer immeasurably because it puts the emphases and pauses where they belong, so all that's left is to translate them into visual signals for the reader.

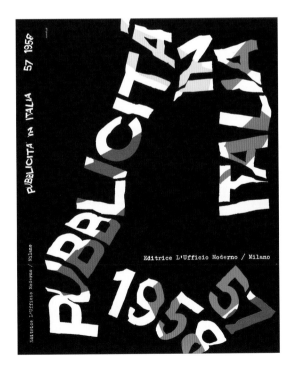

This *process* enlivens the reading experience and produces more effective, more engaging typography. Can this be read, even silently to yourself, without feeling a sense of energy and action? Franco Grignani's book cover and spine for the 1958 *Advertising in Italy* annual uses rephotographed wrinkled type and very intentional allocation of space.

Discussing what type *should* do, Lazar Markovich Lissitzky (better known as El Lissitzky, the Russian avant garde artist, designer, and typographer [1890–1941]) said, *"Typographic arrangement should achieve for the reader what tone of voice conveys for the listener."* This 1924 self-portrait shows he thought of himself as a creative individual, and his 1927 book cover illustrates his philosophy.

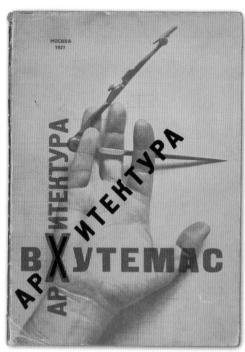

What do we mean by "listening to type"? Imagine listening to an audiobook. The reader's voice changes with the story, helping the listener hear various characters and emotions. ❧ Here, an ad has been deconstructed into copy and three images. The pieces aren't very much to look at, but here's what a type-sensitive designer can do with these pieces.

JET-SMOOTH
Fine-tuned suspension means a smooth ride for you and all your passengers. Now boarding!

The new Toyota Avalon Comfort is back!

Shhhhhh...........
Silence is golden
Sound-absorbing materials.
Reduced wind noise.

Travel Avalon class

Options shown.
©2010 Toyota Motor Sales, USA, Inc.
toyota.com/avalon
Toyota
moving forward

A story told on paper should do the same thing. The "characters" typographers work with are categories of type: headlines, subheads, captions, text, and so forth. These typographic characters are our players and must be matched for both individual clarity and overall unity.

Balancing the intrigue of parts with the cohesion of the whole is perhaps the most difficult and necessary task for a designer. Alignments on left edges, tops of columns, and equalized margins are used to organize the ten individual elements in this pharmaceutical ad.

Typography is, according to the dictionary, "the art or process of printing with type." The root words that make up typography are *typo* (type) and *graphy* (drawing), so it literally means *drawing with type*. My definition is: *Typography: Applying type in an expressive way to reveal the content clearly and memorably with the least resistance from the reader.*

Typography creates clear differences in content, and the differences are valuable even in small, subtle doses. On the left, the bold caption is beneath the text. On the right, note the contrast between text and caption and the subsequent stronger relationship between the caption and the picture, which really does deserve to be exploited.

Typography
The art or process of printing with type

Typo-graphy
type + drawing
Drawing with type

Typography
Applying type
in an expressive way
to reveal content
clearly and memorably
with the least resistance
from the reader

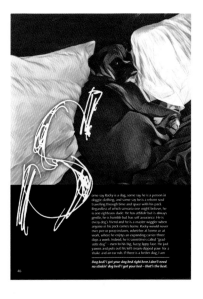
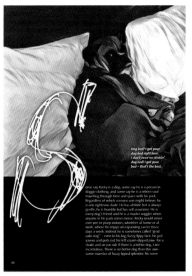

Typography involves far more than working with the abstract black shapes. In practice, typographic decisions are — or should be — 90 percent about the manipulation of the space around the letterforms. This is particularly true if you wish to make negative space — the background — become a figure to be noticed, as in this mark for an art museum.

Good typography results from understanding the importance of the "not-letterforms" and concentrating on both the letter and the spaces between them. This 1952 poster for a Swiss fashion store attends to not-letterforms quite well. The letter-on-letter overlaps have been carefully managed for equivalency and legibility.

Not-letterforms, or the space surrounding letters, is seen between characters, words, and lines and between blocks and columns of type. ❧ It is the contrast of the letterform to its surrounding space that makes type either less or more legible. "Cut The Crap" and "Sorry No Pics Today" are 39-inch squares by Dutch artist Martijn Sandberg.

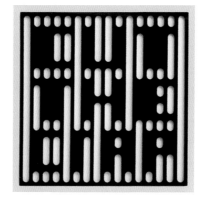

It is not enough to have "nothing wrong" with a design. There must be something recognizably "right" to be considered *good* design. What makes a design less than it can be is a random combination of pieces arranged at whim. Arbitrary font pairings and uncertain positioning make designs sloppy. ❧ Here are the same parts in two studies. Design relationships make designs look predigested and handsome.

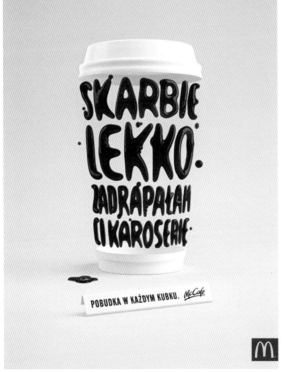

Letterforms can be organic when their role is to convey more than the content of their meaning, as in these hand-lettered figures. The form of the characters — the shape and personality of each word — color our perception of the message (and consequently the product). Spacing between letters and words is crucial in unusual designs: unless they are intentional, visual hiccups may cause readers to avoid a message altogether. The top headline reads "No one learns faster than a masochist" and the bottom reads "Light honey in a full body; Wake up in each cup."

Type, like the spoken voice, can be powerfully bold or elegantly understated. It can warn by shouting or gracefully inform. It can be stuffy or informal, universal or parochial, traditional or state of the art, highly complex or primitive.

Innuendo
Innuendo
Innuendo
Innuendo
Innuendo
Innuendo
Innuendo
Innuendo
INNUENDO

Innuendo
Innuendo
Innuendo
Innuendo
Innuendo
INNUENDO
Innuendo
INNUENDO
Innuendo

Innuendo = Suggestion, Implication, Allusion, Hint

Type's intrigue is often best expressed in combination, as shown in this department spread from *Cargo* magazine. Limited choices are applied to make each bit a separate, short read. But this relatively busy spread holds together as a totality because there are enough similarities to allay the differences.

Sfigato = Unlucky, but not quite the same as disastro magnete

S | F | I | G | A | T | O

Typography may be an art but I'm not an artist.
What can I do to make my type better?

Keep it simple

Infuse it with one distinctive attribute

Don't decorate with type

Make type contrasts big

STANDARDIZE *type specifications and place-ment to build consistency and familiarity. Your readers are well served when things are made to look more alike than more special and unrelated. Apply one of three premade typographic treatments to any story so your readers will see it as either a most important, a least important, or an item of middle importance. The three styles must be related for unity: use the same two typefaces, for example, but vary their size and weights. Contrast serif and sans serif faces, their position, even the spacing beneath each. These alterations signify the content and solidify the design personality by echo-ing design attributes used throughout the document or web site.*

Flavors of type, after Filippo Cecchi, Florence, in 1691: contrasts of size, capitalization, letterspacing, and column width show lively differences. A single type family, Caslon, unites these four voices, balancing their variety with strong consistency.

Typographers use elements and traditions inherited through generations of writing, reading, and printing. Typographic rules, like the development of word spacing, have evolved over centuries. These samples, dating from 400 AD and 569 AD, of square capitals and half uncial handwriting show a lack of word spacing.

Typographic rules, like the adherence to word spacing and default line breaks, may be manipulated to create startling results, as in this contemporary collage painting.

Printable type forms were developed and many typographic rules were adopted from handwriting in the 1400s and 1500s. This is the first italic type ever made. The year was 1501 — it took fifty years after Gutenberg invented movable type — and the visionary was Aldus Manutius, who merely copied the local handwriting style in Venice.

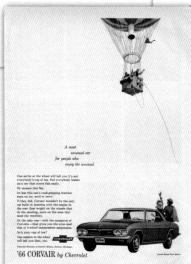

Historically, typography was handled by the printer who cut his own typefaces, designed the page, and reproduced the design on paper (*top, "Book Printer's Shop" by Theodoor Galle, Netherlands, c1595*). In the twentieth century, typography and printing separated. Around 1950, just after World War II, typographers and typesetters became outside vendors who set type to the specifications of the designer or art director, which evolved into a new responsibility. Computers, forcing a new working methodology, have nearly obliterated the typography specialist, since all type decisions are now made within a page design program. Designers are expected to be masters of an art form that takes many years to learn.

Choose a typeface that corresponds to the content. Words are symbols of emotions and ideas that manipulate the reader. Choose letterforms that further and strengthen the brand. These interpretations of corporate logos by Graham Clifford are ad agency J. Walter Thompson's way of thanking its biggest clients at the 150th anniversary of its founding.

Attitude in advertising is often best described using hand lettering. Written language doesn't get much friendlier than this branding. It is a testament to quality art direction that a font wasn't used: except for the nuts.com logo this is all authentically hand lettered.

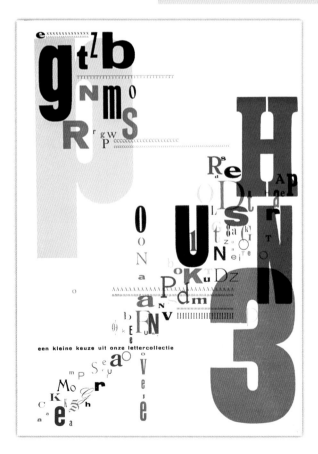

Dutch designer Piet Zwart (1885–1977) was an architect — a designer of three-dimensional space — until age thirty-six, when he turned to typography. Zwart, who called himself a *typotect*, thus approached letterforms unrestrained by then-current design convention. He said, *"Pretentious [letterforms] oppose the utilitarian task of typography. The more uninteresting a letter is in itself the more useful it is in typography."* The danger is that typography will begin and end with choosing a typeface rather than using type to reveal content. And that is not typography, but fashion. Zwart's poster at top is for an Architecture and Applied Arts Exhibition in the Hague (1922). It shows relationships using simple letterforms and space to achieve strict alignments. His page from a 1931 Trio-Reclameboek (Publicity Agency) catalog reads "a small selection from our letter collection" and is a display of the variety of typefaces and sizes available to advertisers. He was very fond of using primary colors.

Keep typography simple

The essence of typography is clarity. R. Hunter Middleton (1898–1985), one of America's most prolific type designers, said, *"Typography is the voice of the printed page. But typography is meaningless until seen by the human eye, translated into sound by the human brain, heard by the human ear, comprehended as thought and stored as memory."* These typefaces were designed by Middleton in the mid- to late 1930s.

Canadian design professor and author Carl Dair wrote, *"Between the two extremes of unrelieved monotony and typographical pyrotechnics there is an area where the designer can contribute to the pleasure of reading and the understanding of what is being read."* "Unrelieved monotony" and "typographic pyrotechnics" describe type treatments that either don't further or actually obscure the message they are meant to convey.

Typographic pyrotechnics are used to slow readers down as they discern the names of recently deceased on a magazine cover. The balance between eye-catching novelty and elegant distinction is necessary on this annual edition, each cover rendered in unique visual poetry.

Establish a tone, a typographic attitude in the display type, where flirtations with reduced legibility are best tolerated by readers. However, unless the reader grasps something of value, his conversion from a *looker* to a *reader* will not occur.

Put interesting information where it can be found. Break the type into palatable chunks. Recognize that readers enter stories through picture captions and respond to ordered information, so have a focal point.

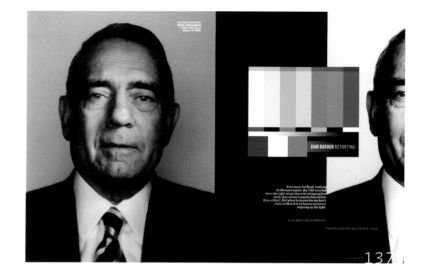

Typographic contrasts express typographic "voices." Legibility can be willingly compromised in order to interpret the meaning of the words. This remarkable calligraphic work carved in stone by John Neilson reads *"Where once was fond and carefree talk cold fear now stills not only words but thought itself."* Any primary type treatment is well served by giving it unique properties.

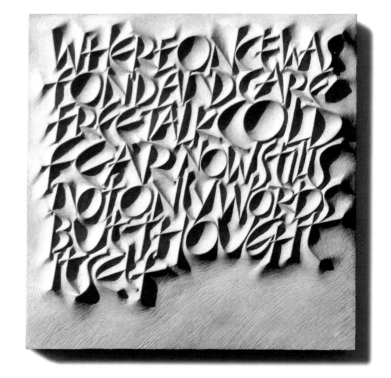

Complexity is much less effective at getting a message across because, though it may be *interesting to look at*, a message with a complex presentation takes more effort to decipher. On the other hand, simplicity alone will not get a message across because, though it may be *easy to read*, its importance won't be recognized. Only simplicity combined with expressiveness will make the message both legible and interesting.

The key to creating expressive typography is to predigest the copy and show off its meaning and its importance to the reader. This can't be separated from the editing process. Read the story, know the subject, ask the client or editor what the thrust ought to be, then make that point crystal clear through design choices.

Abstract word and letter shapes can be manipulated to express meaning as shown in this installation that reads PRETTY UGLY. Such design solutions are born of the attitude that type can be damaged when it is in service to the message.

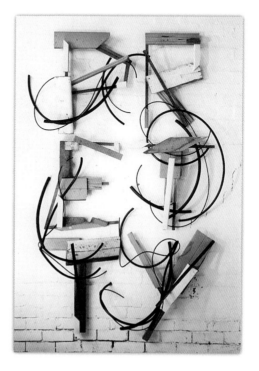

For a design to work effectively, the type must be an integral part of the composition. If the type is altered or removed, the piece should fall apart. It doesn't matter if it's a poster, a cover design, an advertisement, a corporate identity, or an abstract typographic experiment.

Studies in minimal typographic contrast explore the idea of type as frozen sound. This student exercise requires the use of materials from a limited set of samples. This severely limits design opportunities to force creativity so the design, like poetry, merely *hints* at meaning. Experimentation with *form* is the outcome with which we are primarily concerned.

Another student exercise develops design relationships for a poster promoting an annual film festival in California. A neutral sans serif typeface that generously accepts abstraction is assigned, though alternatives may be used if the reason for their use is clear. Imagery is determined by each student but must be related to either the city or film in general. Because this is an advanced typography class, emphasis is placed on type-to-type and type-to-image relationships.

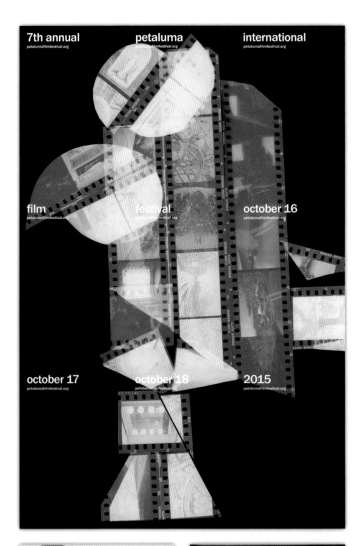

Contrasts of type style, size, weight, position, color, or treatment show hierarchy. Type strategy includes crafting a size and weight sequence through a message so each part is distinctive yet they work as one to make an appealing design. The process of multiple critiques helps designers develop creativity so their work will be notice-able on the crit wall and in the world at large. This is true "value added" design and the essence of what designers *must* bring to their work.

Solidified speech

Good typography effectively translates spoken words into typeset form. Verbal emphasis becomes visual emphasis, most usually by contrast of size or weight. This is the essence of typography: translating the equivalencies of spoken language into printable form.

These expressive variations of a single character in Devangari, used in 120 Indian and Nepalese languages, shows the multiplicity of ways any character can be drawn while retaining its communicative, alphabetic meaning. These are drawn by Sarang Kulkarni, founder of WhiteCrow, a prolific type foundry in Mumbai. Playing around the edges of legibility through experimentation is valuable in adding to one's permanent knowledge.

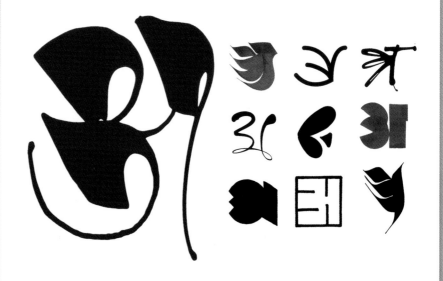

Without this experience, designers are bound to rote adherence to legibility, which is a terrible hindrance to expressive typography, as seen in this award-winning example for a German anti-terrorism poster competition.

ABCDEF GHIJKLM NOPQRST UVWXYZ

ABCDEFGH IJKLMNOP QRSTUVW XYZ

ABCDEFGHIJ KLMNOPQR STUVWYXZ

ABCDEFGHI JKLMNOPQ RSTUVWXYZ 1234567890

ABCDEFGH IJKLMNOP QRSTUVW XYZ

ABCDEFGHI JKLMNOPQR STUVWXYZ

Every typeface has a "visual voice," an equivalency to the spoken word. These alphabets were all designed by Daniel Pelavin and were developed as expansions of typo-illustrations.

ABCDEFGHI JKLMNOPQ RSTUVWYZ

ABCDEFGHI JKLMNOPQR STUVWXYZ

ABCDEFGHI JKLMNOPQ RSTUVWYZ

Treating typography as frozen sound begins with being sensitive to what Gene Federico, a master of advertising design, calls "sound tones." Federico says, "*You must choose a typeface with a sound that isn't against the idea and image you are trying to convey, unless, of course, you are introducing an irritating sound, an irritating typeface for a specific reason.*"

English designer Neville Brody says, "*Let's say a French person comes up to you and starts talking. The first thing you notice is that he's speaking French — not the words that he's said. Just set a piece of text, first in Baskerville* (top at right), *then in several different faces and observe exactly how the message changes. The choice of typeface is critical to the emotional response to the words.*"

Quelle voie vers les toits?

Quelle voie vers les toits?

Quelle voie vers les toits?

Quelle voie vers les toits?

Which way to the rooftops?
Archer Book, Fakir Display Regular, Belo Script, Baskerville Old Face Regular

INVIDI

ICIANI

Developing sensitivity to rhythm is also important. Rhythm requires breaking repetition, which creates visual surprise and a focal point. While this mark is a splendid example of rhythm, note that some capital letters have been abstracted and, when read upside down, can be misread. *INVIDI*, the actual name of the company, is not the same as *ICIANI*.

In his most brilliant speech On the Crown one of the most splendid political pleas ever written Demosthenes not only defended Ctesiphon but also attacked vehemently those who would have preferred peace with Macedon In this trial Demosthenes' entire political career was at issue, but the orator repudiated nothing of what he had done He begins with a general view of the condition of Greece when he entered politics and describes the phases of his struggle

In his most brilliant speech *On the Crown*, one of the most splendid political pleas ever written, **Demosthenes** not only defended **Ctesiphon** but also attacked vehemently those who would have *preferred peace with Macedon.* In this trial, Demosthenes' **entire political career** was at issue, but the orator *repudiated nothing* of what he had done. He begins with a *general view* of the condition of Greece

A speaker who drones at a single speed is causing his listeners extra work to dig out the good content. By comparison, a speaker who alters the rhythm of delivery, by pausing before beginning a new idea, for example, makes the content clearer by grouping information into sensible clusters. Type is frozen sound, so attend to visual rhythm and pauses.

Rhythm can be enhanced typographically by breaking the ends of lines of *display type* in surprising places, rather than whenever a line happens to be filled with letterforms, as is common and generally appropriate with *text* settings. Breaking words unexpectedly produces quirky, unconventional messages.

If the line of display type is broken arbitrarily or broken in the wrong place, reading and comprehension is slowed down. If natural line breaks don't work well visually, editing the copy, adjusting the layout, or changing typefaces may be necessary.

Badly broken headlines

When eating an elephant, take one bite at a time.

Almost anything is easier to get into than out of.

Those who are most moral are farthest from the problem.

Don't force it, get a larger hammer.

Some of it plus the rest of it is all of it.

Well broken headlines

When eating an elephant, take one bite at a time.

Almost anything is easier to get into than out of.

Those who are most moral are farthest from the problem.

Don't force it, get a larger hammer.

Some of it plus the rest of it is all of it.

Punctuation (as in this full-page newspaper ad), capitalization, and extra word spacing can make a headline, in effect, a typographic illustration. Do whatever is necessary to serve the reader's interest in having information look predigested.

One last thought on the importance of space on type: Emil Ruder, the Swiss designer, teacher, and author, said, *"The quality of typography is dependent on the relationship between the printed and the unprinted parts. It is a sign of professional immaturity to ignore the decisive contribution of the unprinted area."*

External limitations compel and shape creativity. Embrace them. Not having constraints makes decisions harder: How can you know what is best when there are so many stones left unturned?

Interpret constraints as creative opportunities.

How a Logo Fits into a Company's Branding Strategy

Chapter 4

The logo is the most significant visual element in a branding plan, and it must signify the company's essence. Like clothing, it is a company's "public dress."

A logo provides viewers with a symbol of the consistent experience of a product or service. ❧ This chapter will discuss the part that a logo plays in a client's overall branding and will look at three topics from the designer's point of view.

Marketing Strategies What an identity is and how to manage its perception; **Research and Planning an Identity** How the job brief sets a measurable target and promotes creativity; and **The Elements of a Successful Identity** Including appropriateness, recognition, clichés, and value of compliance.

This chapter describes the context and position of the logo in a company's drive to brand product. It is the introduction to the final three chapters "How to Build a Logo, Parts 1, 2, and 3," which discuss how to design a logo to reveal a company's essence.

What makes a logo "good"? A good logo must, of course, be good on its own design merits — it has inherent æsthetic quality, which is a balance between artistry, inventiveness, and elegance.

A "good" logo must be good for the client by satisfying the brand positioning and by meeting clearly stated business objectives.

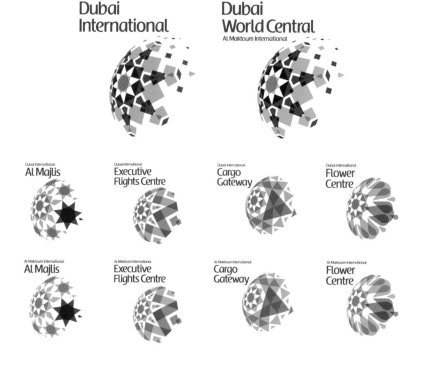

A "good" logo lasts for at least ten years. Logo design is solving limited design relationships in an especially consequential mark.

A logo has two jobs: it represents the company in tone and character by distilling abstract thoughts into representational style, and it is the primary visual element and informs all subsequent design treatments.

Marketing Strategies
Logos are a significant component to brand building — and brands ought not be invisible. Making something visible requires taking a risk to stand out: this is both a daring business decision and the designer's challenge.

The visual impression a company makes is one part of an overall experience of a company or product. To expect too much from a logo is unrealistic.

OCULUS

To many clients, "design" is optional surface decoration to make things look nice. Counteract this by defining real branding problems and solving them. Decoration is "surface"; design is "solution." These preliminary studies and final mark explore both the visible design relationships and the tone or character the client wants to project for a mom-and-pop shop that sells gummies from around the world.

The goal of branding is to create empathy and attachment to a company by having it stand for something and to give customers a consistent experience with every interaction.

Identity is a business suit

An identity is the "trade dress" that creates a consistent experience of a company (which may become boring to the company well before it does to the audience). An identity is the physical manifestation or representation of the *idea* of a company. The *experience* of a company — as its customers perceive it — is its *brand*.

Brand perception and position

A brand is a cumulative experience of a company in the minds of its customers. The experience is built on consistent, multisensory messages that reveal what the company or product stands for and its position relative to its competitors. In his book *The Brand Gap*, Marty Neumeier says, "*Brand is not just a logo attached to a product or company.*"

**A BRAND IS NOT WHAT YOU SAY IT IS.
A BRAND IS WHAT THEY SAY IT IS.**

MARTY NEUMEIER

He continues, "*Brand is not an identity… Brand is a symbol of choices made on behalf of a product: philosophy, experience, quality, lifestyle, aspirations, status, desire, power, and achievement. Branding helps customers understand a product and what it wants to be for them. A brand is a person's gut feeling about a product, service, or organization.*" ❧ In short, brand is not what *you* say it is. Brand is what *targets* say it is.

Let's talk about brand position. How is the company trying to express itself? How does it see itself, and how does it want others to see it? What is the client trying to express? Where does the company fit in the marketplace of competing products and services? How does it think of itself in that milieu — and how does the company want others to think of it?

Martin Lindstrom writes in his book *Buy-ology: Truth and Lies About Why We Buy* that brand perception is measurable. MRI brain scans from 2,000 subjects from around the world show that the human brain perceives and reacts in the exact same way to images of religious icons and widely known brands, logos, products, ads, and television commercials. This chart shows levels of positive and negative emotions.

LOYALTY

TRUST

AUTHENTICITY

CONSISTENCY

POSITIVE INTERACTIONS

NEGATIVE INTERACTIONS

INCONSISTENCY

INAUTHENTICITY

DISTRUST

DISLOYALTY

A German study in 2008 shows that familiar brands are processed in a part of the brain that processes positive emotions. Unfamiliar brands take more effort to recognize and are processed in an area of the brain that handles negative emotions.

Getting your clients' brands into the part of their targets' brains that is positive takes time and money. Familiarity is the result, and familiarity has financial value.

Define and develop a unique standing
Who is in your client's business community? What makes your client a viable business entity? Show that in their business dress, either abstractly or very specifically, depending on the global scale of the business. Organic growth is interpreted "locally" above and "globally" below.

Robin Rutherford, DDS

Local businesses may need a more literal, specific mark that show their product or service. Global businesses may be better served by a more abstract mark.

The ultimate unique standing is known as a "charismatic brand." Charisma means "a compelling charm that inspires devotion in others; charming, fascinating; magnetic, captivating, beguiling, alluring." A charismatic brand draws *fans*, not just customers. A charismatic brand, then, is the best kind of brand to be: it is a product, service, or organization for which customers believe there is no substitute.

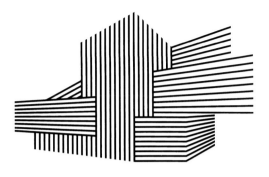

If you want to stand out, you have to have distinctive design. Neutral design is forgettable. But be quirky in a way that promotes the client's true character and is memorable.

BLACKSTONE

Your client has two audiences: direct competitors and the business community at large. It is essential to differentiate your client from direct competitors and it is wise to differentiate your client in the greater business community. Know your mark's potential to stand out in the general population of similar shapes.

Research your client's competitors' marks to avoid accidental similarity. What shapes, colors, and letterforms do they use? Don't rely on your client for sourcing this information. Show this collection of competitors' logos for context prior to presenting your studies: it will make your work look even better. Know your mark's potential in the specific marketplace of similar businesses.

Google makes researching logo shapes very easy. In the face of so many competitive marks, to come up with something uniquely new and appropriate for your client is challenging. Just remember that to be hip is to follow the crowd, but to be visible is to design against current trends.

"Brand" is not "logo"

"Brand" is more like "identity." It is a calculated cumulative perception based on various contact points, including your use of the product, your experience of the product, the history of the product, the way your friends think of the product, and, of course, the logo, which is the icon of the product. A logo is the visual description or interpretation of a brand. "Brand" is the difference between the actual cheese inside the wrapper and your perception of a difference between, say, D'Amir over Cello Riserva or Taleggio DOP. (DOP, incidentally, stands for *Denominazione di Origine Protetta* or "Protected Designation of Origin," assuring the Italian product is locally grown and packaged.)

Logos are flags personifying the sponsor. A logo promises that the advertiser has approved the ad, that it gives an accurate presence of the company, and that the advertiser stands by what the ad says. Logo placement in ads is typically in the lower right corner, geographically the last place in a multistop message that proceeds through a visual, a primary headline, often a secondary headline, the text, and finally the logo.

What does a logo do? It identifies the origin — the manufacturer or provider — of the product or service. In addition, a logo differentiates one company from its competition and creates an identity and an experience that points outward to customers and inward to employees. This early 1960s ad campaign was so consistently designed that one ad could intentionally leave out the recognizability of the car *and* the sponsor's logo.

A good logo creates an emotional reaction. In the best circumstances, it ends up being worn and voluntarily adopted for free advertising by those who identify with the brand.

A good logo is *original*. Originality can generally be found by solving a very well-defined problem. Indeed, when a visual problem has been fully and completely defined, the solution always presents itself. You just have to notice it when it shows itself. A bad logo lacks its own character and creates the response that "it looks familiar."

What precisely is a "logo"?
This is what Google says are logos, but identifying marks have been around since about 15,000 BC. Personal identifying marks appeared in about 6,000 BC, perhaps just after the idea of "ours" was replaced by "mine" and "yours." Merchants' marks became common about 800 years ago, identifying products with symbols that could be understood by people who couldn't read. Logos used in the modern sense were developed during the Industrial Revolution in the late 1800s when manufacturing processes changed dramatically, expanding sales of mass-produced goods.

15,000 BC   4,000 BC   1,200 AD   c. 1880

"Logo"

- **Greek for "word"**
- **Symbol that identifies a company's product**
- **Synonyms: *trademark, emblem, device, figure, signature***

The dictionary says a logo, short for *logotype* and from the Greek for "word," is "a symbol or other small design to identify a company's products. Synonyms include *trademark* (a legally registered and protected mark), *emblem*, *device*, *figure*, and *signature*." That definition is both too vague and too comprehensive for a logo designer's needs, so let's clarify it as simply as possible:

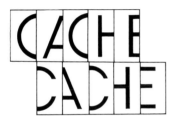

EVOLUZIONE EDILIZIA

"Mark," the parent term for four subgroups, is a visual device showing origin or ownership.

- ➲ **Symbol**, an icon or a mark without type,
- ➲ **Lettermark**, an unreadable monogram,
- ➲ **Logo** or **logotype**, a readable word; a term incorrectly applied to all marks, and
- ➲ **Combination mark**, a symbol joined with a lettermark or logo.

Research and Planning an Identity

Design is much harder than merely giving clients what they ask for. It takes vision and creativity to turn an obvious set of criteria (what good clients provide) into a fresh, memorable, "creative" expression of the real, underlying problem. The given problem — your assignment — must be turned inside out.

Implying the gutter of a magazine spread in the type area of a one-page ad could only have come from a designer who is seeking fresh ways of showing the familiar. Anything less than interpreting the given problem and adding real intellectual value is a concession that a nondesigner's untrained imagination is adequate. Absent a custom-crafted solution, the client's thought becomes more solidified that the expense of a designer is not essential.

This year, the most colorful gifts are coming in black and white. Copper Centerpiece Bowl, $39.95.
For the store nearest you, call 800 996 9960. crateandbarrel.com

Design is the marriage of a need and its expressive solution. It takes certain vision from the client and clear vision from designers to achieve branding excellence. This wonderful set of stickers with its hidden negative space iconography is provided by the Coca-Cola company.

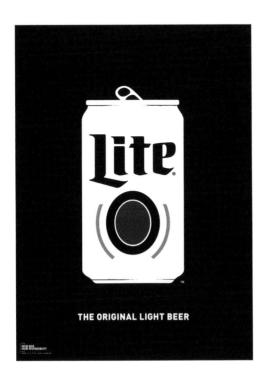

Most clients start out sincerely wanting fresh, innovative, and noticeable design, then dilute it during multiple meetings until the result is familiar, ordinary, expected, and frustrating for everyone. The client thinks, "If I'd hired a *good* designer, I'd have gotten better work." The designer thinks, "If only they had left well enough alone, it wouldn't have gotten familiarized down to mediocrity." This ad's simplicity clearly survived the process.

When planning an identity, be sure it represents the company. Ask them to provide some research (they know more about their business than you do) and samples of marks and other design they do like. Without this spadework, you are unlikely to avoid frustration: you are stabbing in the dark. This mark is an interpretation of a distinctively shaped building in New York City.

In addition to asking for client preferences, know both the direct and more general competition and how they are presenting themselves: know what direction the traffic is going so your work can stand out. If you are working on the identity for a new building, it is essential to know how other buildings are being represented.

Client needs and preferences

As an outside consultant, quickly get to know your client's business as well as you can. If you are on staff, you already have knowledge of what is wanted — though that may be as much a limitation as an opportunity. The more you know about what is wanted and what is liked, the better you'll be able to hit the sweet spot early in the process.

Educate your client in the predesign work of defining her preferences and her goals, which saves you time going down blind alleys. Press a client to give you tear sheets of likes and dislikes, and don't limit it just to other logos she's seen. More examples are better than only a few.

Another predesign process is a **brand audit**, an assessment of the brand's strengths and weaknesses in the company's brand-building tools. The audit identifies what is being done and whether it is effective. Begin by exploring these four questions.

- **Is the brand projecting a consistent voice?**
- **What is the brand's promise?**
- **Who is the primary audience?**
- **How can the brand be better positioned?**

There is **brand equity**, years of investment in the existing branding that must be protected and may be exploited for evolutionary growth. Cashing in this equity for frivolous reasons is not a good idea.

1901   1930s   1946   1970

A couple of tips on handling clients: what clients say and what they mean are generally very different. They don't know what they want until they see what they don't want. So show examples consistently. Like an ophthalmologist flipping lenses, ask, "This . . . or this?" Be ready to verbally describe the visual ideas you are presenting, so your work isn't judged on whether it is "liked" but on how well it satisfies the agreed-to objectives.

Be politically savvy by taking what you might think is a bad client suggestion and making it better. There is a kernel of usefulness in everything: find it and craft it into something useful. Twisting an externally sourced idea into something new is a great route to a fresh result.

A thorough creative brief *causes* the solution

Before solving a problem, it must be defined in clear terms. A **creative brief** is a written document that comprehensively and concisely defines the business problem that you will solve. *Its purpose is to reduce subjectivity.* Creatives should take an active role in the development of the brief. The designer's task is to progress from a single *strategy* to a few *concepts* to multiple *executions*.

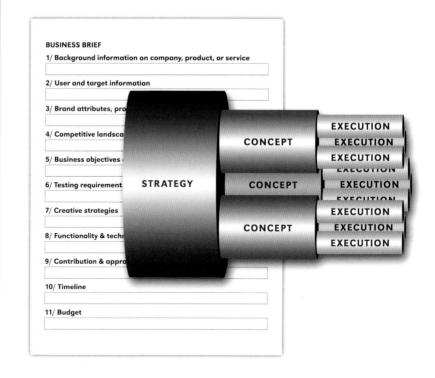

The elements of a creative brief are:

Background information on the company, product, or service

- ⊃ User and target audience groups
- ⊃ Brand attributes, promise, and mission
- ⊃ Competitive landscape
- ⊃ Who are we selling to? Who are we selling against? What will our product do for the user? What are the key benefits?

BUSINESS BRIEF

1/ Background information on company, product, or service

2/ User and target information

3/ Brand attributes, promise, and mission

4/ Competitive landscape

5/ Business objectives & success criteria

6/ Testing requirements & measurement of success

7/ Creative strategies

8/ Functionality & technical specifications

9/ Contribution & approval process

10/ Timeline

11/ Budget

What are the facts about the subject and its audience?

BUSINESS BRIEF

1/ Background information on company, product, or service

2/ User and target information

3/ Brand attributes, promise, and mission

4/ Competitive landscape

5/ **Business objectives & success criteria**

6/ **Testing requirements & measurement of success**

7/ **Creative strategies**

8/ **Functionality & technical specifications**

9/ **Contribution & approval process**

10/ **Timeline**

11/ **Budget**

What are the objectives and how will they be tested?

Business objectives and success criteria

↻ Testing requirements and measurement of success

↻ Creative strategies

↻ What is the key fact, the one thing the design must accomplish? How will the design affect the user's attitudes o behavior? How will the design's success be measured?

BUSINESS BRIEF

1/ Background information on company, product, or service

2/ User and target information

3/ Brand attributes, promise, and mission

4/ Competitive landscape

5/ Business objectives & success criteria

6/ Testing requirements & measurement of success

7/ Creative strategies

8/ **Functionality & technical specifications**

9/ **Contribution & approval process**

10/ **Timeline**

11/ **Budget**

How many rounds, who is the contact, when are parts due, and how much will it cost?

Functionality and technical specifications

↻ Contribution and approval process

↻ Timelines

↻ Budget

↻ Musts and must-nots in client and agency preferences. Defining the number of rounds of revisions and a single point of contact will cause clients to focus the process.

Know your audience

What makes your audience — your *client's* audience — different than people in general? What makes them respond? Unless you are designing for other designers, there are going to be important differences between what *you* think is good and what *they* will find persuasive.

Those differences, once uncovered, will provide terrific grip when starting your sketches: defining *this* problem's unique requirements leads to unique solutions. Because of cultural and language differences, global audiences may need a more abstract mark than local or national audiences. Large branding companies have specialists that research and avoid cultural errors.

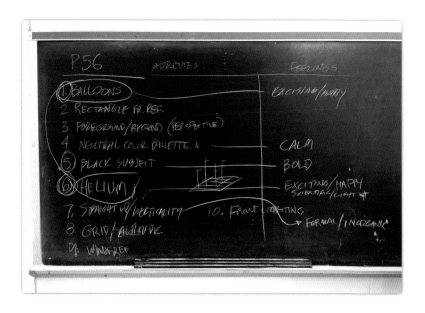

Process thinking

Don't start a design without an objective. Have you ever sat in front of the screen just making digital doodles? It's very time consuming and ultimately a fruitless process. Pencil and paper first, silicon chip second. And refer often to the well-written job brief to be sure you are on course.

Clichés become clichés because they are such good illustrations of an idea. Be very watchful for using a common, overused idea. At the very least, give an old idea a fresh spin — and be alert that even your "fresh spin" has probably already been done. Clients deserve a mark *they alone can own.*

Including elements of surprise in a design is highly effective. "Surprise" is another word for "creative" and creativity is mostly perspiration, not inspiration.

Research the client, turn leaves, try combinations. Use words to jumpstart visuals. Don't settle for *okay* when *great* is around the corner.

Process sketches

Quantity absolutely leads to *quality*. Sketch 50, 100, even 300 notions quickly to release clichés and explore with a sense of fun and silliness. Sketch away from your normal work environment: you will think differently in a different environment. I do some of my best visualizing on the commuter train into New York City and on the subway under Manhattan.

Once you have enough sketches, begin solidifying them into more definitive studies. Never show work you don't like. It's almost universally followed: the study you like the least will be chosen by your client. And it's too late to change at that point. So *if you don't love it, the client shouldn't see it.*

Show the fewest studies possible: four to seven in phase 1. The more studies you present, the more random your process looks to the client. Portray yourself as a *problem-solver* rather than a stylist. ❋ Some elite designers believe in showing one solution for one problem. That is a principled extreme that probably won't work for most designers who haven't yet developed gigantic reputations, but the thinking behind it is admirable.

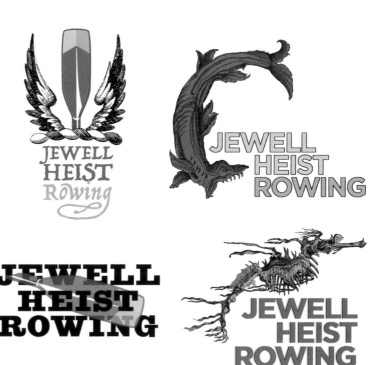

The final study shows a continuous evolution in type color. The playful result further differentiates this club from others, which is a consideration at regattas where identities become acutely attended to.

Circle-R, TM, and SM
Designing a mark is only half the job. The client typically isn't satisfied until the mark has been reproduced hundreds, thousands, millions of times for his audience. But developing a brand requires that its elements can't be snagged by competitors, so having legal claim to its parts is essential.

Calipia®

Calipia®

Calipia®

Calipia®

If a mark is insufficiently distinct, it can't be protected from infringement by others. It is important to note that an unprotectable mark has no value. A mark that isn't aggressively protected from infringement loses its value if it is copied or plagiarized by others. The top two studies are merely typeset. The bottom two have distinctive treatments that make them more protectable.

Branding elements that can be trademarked are: name, visual mark, tagline, package, product design, page treatment, shape, color or combination of colors, and even a sound that identifies and distinguishes the source from those of others. *Make any of these most protectable by making the mark as distinctive as possible.* The more differentiated it is from its competitors, the better.

Calipia®

Calipia® = e-world™

MPEG 4

CalipiaRoosterCall.m4a

What's the difference between these typographic "bugs"? **Circle-R** (®) stands for *Registered Trademark* and indicates that the mark has been registered with the US or another federal government. This is the strongest legal protection available. Each of these examples is the same type size: some fonts have Circle-R marks that are the correct size for the type being used, and others need to be designated as superscript.

® TM SM

Access the Circle-R mark at keystroke option-r

The TM mark is generally not available as a pre-made glyph. You have to make it yourself and size it.

TM TM TM **TM** TM *TM* TM TM TM TM ***TM*** **TM** *TM* TM TM

TM TM TM TM **TM** TM **TM** TM TM **TM** **TM** TM TM

TM **TM** TM **TM** TM TM TM TM TM TM **TM** TM TM **TM**

TM *TM* TM TM *TM* TM TM TM TM TM **TM** TM TM TM

Гео® Гео™ Гео SM

CAP HEIGHT

BASELINE

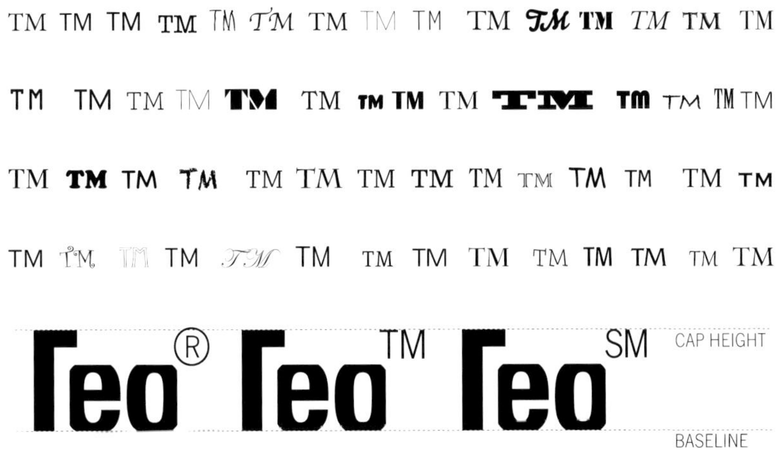

TM (™) stands for *Trademark* and is a claim of ownership for a design that does not have federal recognition for its use. It is therefore comparatively weak protection but is useful as a sign of prior use and ownership in case of legal action. ❀ This diagram shows the correct location and sizes for placing the Circle-R, Trademark, and Service Marks.

The SM mark is also not available as a pre-made glyph. You have to make it yourself and size it.

SM SM SM **SM** SM *SM* SM SM SM SM ***SM*** **SM** *SM* SM SM

SM SM SM SM **SM** SM **SM** SM SM **SM** **SM** SM SM

SM **SM** SM **SM** SM SM SM SM SM SM **SM** SM SM **SM**

SM *SM* SM SM *SM* SM SM SM SM SM **SM** SM SM SM

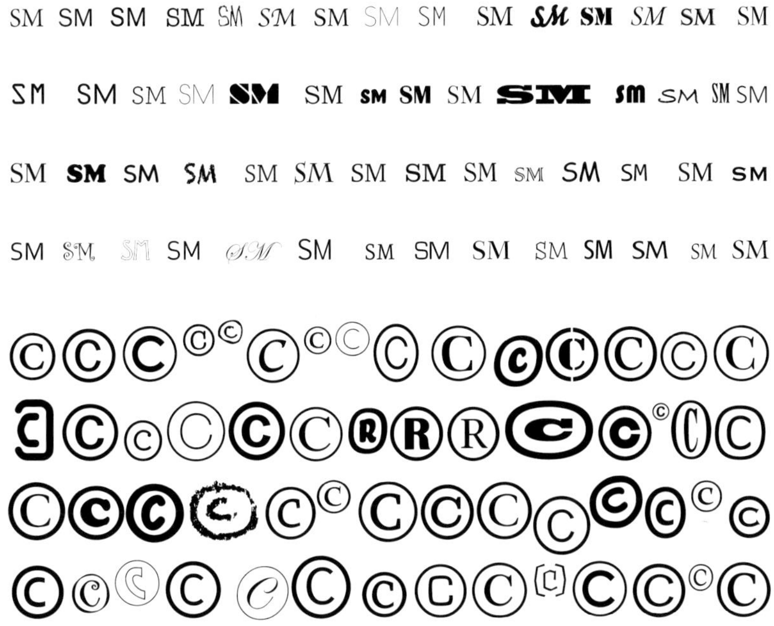

SM (℠) stands for *Service Mark* and is a claim of ownership for a unique service. ❀ There are other legal protections that do not typically apply to marks and branding elements:

    Circle-C (©) stands for *Copyright* and protects artistic and literary work; and

    A **patent** protects an invention, though it has no glyph to indicate that protection.

The Elements of a Successful Identity

Every company — and seemingly every individual businessperson — wants a mark that represents their brand, the business experience they offer. In this raucous environment, it is harder and harder to be recognized. This is the population of marks in a single recent issue of a weekly news magazine.

A successful identity requires a reference, whether it is representational or abstract, to the core business.

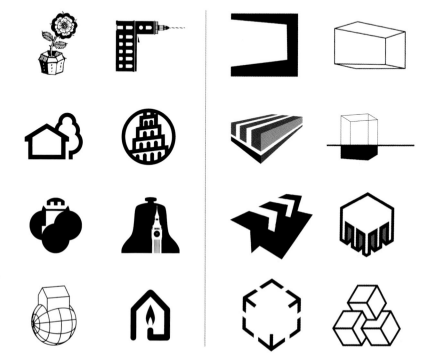

A successful identity requires unique, noticeable design. When representing a company with a word mark, the letterforms used are crucial to the mark's unique recognizability. The client's name is typeset in eight evocative faces, none of which have been adjusted or customized to create a true brand mark. The bottom mark was hand drawn by Georg Trump and, as an original artwork, is positively unique. This is an example of calligraphy ("beautiful writing") being rougher and more expressive, i.e., less traditional, than one might anticipate. That kind of freshness is needed for every client.

Nicolas Jenson Italic   Pelican
Poppl-Residenz Script   Preissig Kursiva
Ruzicka Freehand   Snell Roundhand
Trattatello   Wilke Bold Italic
Handdrawn by Georg Trump

Character, consistently used, makes an identity successful. Identifying the character you want to convey — character that is borne out by every other branding message — is the role of the job brief and the subsequent *design strategy*, *concepts*, and *executions*.

- **A great idea simplified to its essence**
- **Knowledgeable management of content**
- **Precise relationships**
- **Exact spacing**
- **Elegant execution**

A successful identity grows organically out of the unique aspects of *this* client in *this* business with *these* people. The designer carries the intellectual and cultural responsibility of giving visible form to thoughts and ideas.

 surepoint  surepoint

surepoint surepoint

surepoint

Appropriate idea
An appropriate design idea reveals the essence of a business with *maximum character* and, often, *with more than a single layer of meaning.* Inappropriate ideas occur because the designer can't help but take a stab at executing a neat new technique, or outdoing colleagues, or by falling in love with an early idea and not exploring the real problem more deeply. Clients are right to expect true originality.

Me-too thinking, clichés, and, contemptibly, theft
Marks are susceptible to movements and changing fashions. Designers rarely accept that notion at the moment, but it becomes clear in hindsight. Defining your clients' business in a trendy set of clothes is not helpful: to the degree those clothes are in fashion and of-the-moment, they will become out of fashion in short order. Timelessness and appropriateness survive trends.

It is more than a little embarrassing to design a mark that already exists. It can happen to anyone who doesn't do research: NBC paid a lot to develop a new network logo (*left*). One design was chosen and fully implemented. Then it was discovered that the station manager at Nebraska Educational Television, a PBS affiliate, had designed and been using that exact lettermark (*right*) for his small-market television station.

Try to design something new, not simply new to you. Clients and marketing personnel are bound to love the familiar, so take their responses and rework your idea to accommodate their contributions while at the same time providing originality.

Recognition without reading

A logo's shape should be recognizable without having to actually read the mark. A logo doesn't have to be conspicuous to do its job. Clients sometimes think making the logo large is a bet against targets who don't read the ad or pay attention to any other part of the message. They may be right, but that is a failing of the rest of the message, not necessarily a measure of success of the logo.

All logos are symbolic and abstract to some degree. Pablo Picasso's studies in abstraction, done over a six-week period, show a progressive investigation into the purest essence of a bull. Without the first studies, how difficult is it to recognize the animal in the last two studies? The more abstract a mark is, the more it takes repeated contact — an investment in time and money — to get an audience to recognize and remember the mark.

12.05.45	12.12.45	12.18.45
12.22.45	12.24.45	12.26.45
12.28.45	01.02.46	01.05.46
01.10.46	01.17.46	*FINIS.*

Smaller, local businesses tend to have more literal, less abstract marks. Conglomerates and global entities and companies whose businesses can't be easily illustrated benefit from more abstract marks.

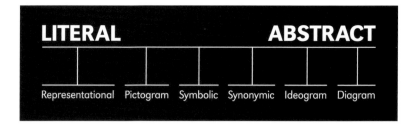

Compliance cop

Consistent use of the logo and all visual elements is the cornerstone of building brand recognition. It is this aspect of designing on staff in a company that becomes most tedious, but it is necessary for the development and sustainability of the product's visual presence. "Design standards" are described in a style manual that shows what should and should not be done with a mark.

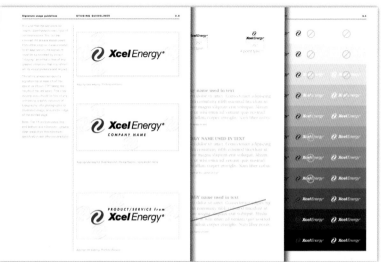

Taglines

A tagline or *slogan* is a succinct, striking, emotive compression of a brand's message. Logos with companion taglines are ordinarily the last part of a message, and while they are in fact two separate elements, they must be designed so they are perceived as a single entity.

Alina Wheeler writes in *Designing Brand Identity*, "The tagline is a short phrase that captures a company's brand essence, personality, and positioning, and distinguishes it from its competitors. . . A tagline must be short, it must capture the brand essence and positioning, it must be easy to say and remember, it evokes an emotional response, and it can be protected with trademark." There are four kinds of taglines, as shown here.

Descriptive *Describes service, product, or brand promise*

Allstate	You're in good hands
GE	Imagination at work
Philips	Sense and simplicity
Subway	Eat fresh
KFC	Finger-lickin' good!
Morton Salt	When it rains, it pours
Frosted Flakes	They're g-r-r-r-eat!
Avis	We try harder
Kay Jewelers	Every kiss begins with Kay

Imperative *Commands action, usually starts with a verb*

AmEx	Don't leave home without it
Nike	Just do it
Prudential	Get a piece of the rock
Walmart	Save money. Live better.
Lay's	Betcha can't eat just one
Marlboro	Come to Marlboro Country
Target	Expect more. Pay less.
Honda	Simplify

Provocative *Thought-provoking, often as a question*

Capital One	What's in your wallet?
Dairy Council	Got milk?
McDonald's	I'm lovin' it
Clairol	Does she or doesn't she?

Superlative *Positions the company as best in category*

Filson	Might as well have the best
L'Oréal	Because you're worth it
U.S. Marines	The few. The Proud.
Stella Artois	Reassuringly expensive
Nestlé	Good food. Good life.
M&M's	Melts in your mouth, not in your hands
Budweiser	The king of beers
Meow Mix	Tastes so good, cats ask for it by name
John Deere	Nothing runs like a Deere
DeBeers	A diamond is forever
Wheaties	Breakfast of Champions
Bounty	The quicker picker upper

Using this rule forces you to attend to space without complacency. Default spacing in any area of design is for casualists. Practice seeing positive and negative forms with *equal* skepticism.

Spacing is never perfect. It is either too open or too tight.

Chapter 5

The most basic logos use only letterforms and space. These all-type marks are some of John Langdon's ambigrams, readable upside down, that show the flexibility of letterforms and brilliant use of space.

A logo, like all graphic design, is made of three ingredients: type, image, and space. Without space as a full partner in type and space marks, a logo is merely typesetting. In logo design, *as in all design*, the most interesting solutions occur in the places where the three ingredients overlap. It is sometimes easiest to determine what a design element is by identifying the two it is *not*.

A logo must signify a company's *essence*. All of these marks are designed by Lief Frimann Anisdahl, a central figure in Norwegian graphic design. Try to identify which are only type and space. In the process, you may be surprised to discover that *imagery* is the key determinant. In this chapter, we will be concerned only with two of the three elements: type and space — and of course where type or space can *become each other*.

There are four aspects of the type and space logo:
Anatomy of a Type and Space Logo and the parts that can be used to build one.
Figure (Letterform)–Ground Relationship and how to make them ambiguous and interchangeable.
Letterforms, Type, and Fonts, the differences between them, and why it matters.
Type Alteration including abstraction and legibility.

Anatomy of a Type and Space Logo

The term "logo" is commonly and incorrectly applied to *any* mark, but "logo" really has a very specific meaning. A logo (or **logotype** or **wordmark**) is properly and only a mark that is a readable word. These are proper logos.

These are **lettermarks** or **monograms**, unpronounceable names formed by letters.

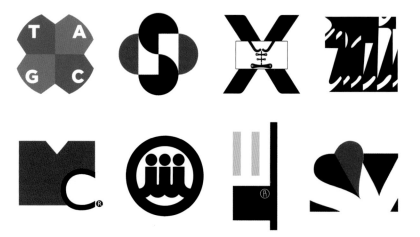

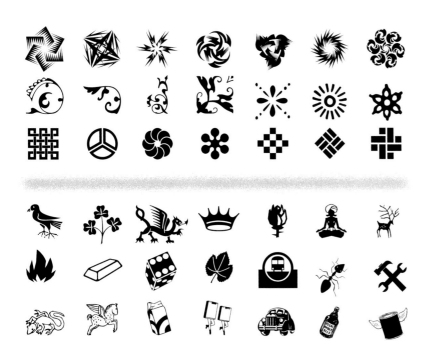

These are **symbols**, nonread-able marks of varying realism. A symbol can be an **arbitrary mark**, which is nonrepresenta-tional or a common word used in an unrelated context, or a symbol can be an **icon**, which is a more illustrative visual symbol.

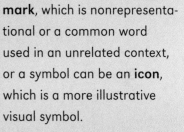

CITY ONE

These are **combination marks**, symbols joined to lettermarks or logos.

Lastly, **trademarks** (or **brandmarks**) are any of the previously listed marks that are *legally protected*.

A mark can be made of an image or symbol and readable or nonreadable letterforms, plus — in either case — space.

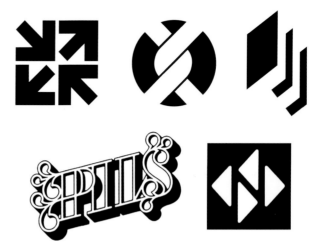

Secondary type can be added, for example a tagline or brief description of the company. These pieces are not necessarily always present as a group: any of the pieces can appear alone or in combination. *But* consistency is essential to produce a repeated effect on an audience.

The success of a logo's design is dependent on the pieces — mark, primary type, and secondary type — being integrated into a *single design entity.*

Two or three unrelated pieces that happen to be near to one another is not a mark, it is merely a *thing*. Nothing has been done to make these three pieces work as one, aside from their nearness to one another and their shared black color. If a design doesn't have evident design *relationships*, it is fair to say it isn't a design.

Crafting or forcing shared design attributes makes the difference between a *thing* and a designed mark. Here are two variations showing developed design relationships.

The Figure (Letterform)–Ground Relationship

The relationship of figure to ground is the most fundamental relationship in all of design. The strongest indication of whether a designer is good is the way they handle space as a legitimate shape, treated equally to the shapes of the figures in it.

Use of ground, or white space, is particularly important in logo design, where there are so few relationships crammed into what should be a tiny jewel of design perfection.

To be good at logo design, a designer has to have learned *how to see background as foreground* and learned how to make the two grounds ambiguous and interchangeable.

Using space can also be expressed by judiciously removing it, as in this mark carved in stone by Annet Stirling. That the apparent overlapping letters transparency is trompe l'œil *in real stone* is the magic here. The authentic dimensional crafting adds immeasurably to its character. Replicating it digitally cheapens the effect and is not a true substitute.

33
REITVELDT

In relatively unsophisticated type-and-space logo designs, *type is type* and *space* is, by default, *"not type,"* the unnoticed areas *behind* the type. These marks can be attractive and distinctive but without active negative space they will not be exceptional.

eronen

Richer design solutions are achieved when type and space become a bit more ambiguous: *type is space* and *space is type*. This requires *abstraction* so our eyes don't automatically glom onto only the letters. The turntable is also a lowercase "e."

Activate space by making its shapes as interesting and thoughtfully crafted as the figures in it. Force us to perceive the ground as well as the figures by disguising the figures, which are the *familiar* shapes.

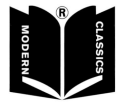

The interaction of figure and ground is explored in this single simple form, a 1485 blackletter "S." The progression shows increasing variations that assign a different shade to each shape — ignoring which shapes are part of the letter and which are part of the background. The result is a lot more playful and unexpected — and all we did was ignore routine figure/ground assignments.

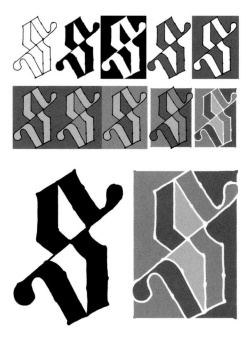

The MG lettermark on the left appears to ignore letterspacing. But in the middle study we can see the negative shapes have been given equal and very careful consideration. In a detail of the mark on the right, we see that the thick-thin-thick line quality adds character through rhythm.

Letterspacing, the space between characters, is perceived as ground because it appears "behind" the letterforms. Here, the letterspacing has been mightily compromised between the letters "I," "V," "A," and "M," and the baselines are topsy-turvy to create extreme abstraction — and a *recognizable*, if unreadable, mark for a Spanish magazine. In the extracted letterforms we see the letters are three sizes but otherwise unchanged — only the ground has been manipulated.

Letterforms, Type, and Fonts

In this section, we will consider the difference between these three kinds of visible language and why it matters. ❦ **Letterforms** are the shapes of the characters, *separate from how they are made or reproduced.* The letterforms we use have developed over thirty-five centuries, shaped by world history and commerce, scientific development, and simple preference. A letterform maintains its integrity whether it is drawn with pen on paper, cut and pasted in Photoshop, or typeset as outline files in a font. Those techniques do affect the way the letterform is transmitted and perceived. ❦ Frederic W. Goudy did these studies to show the development of letterforms (*top*) and variety of each letter in his book *The Alphabet and Elements of Lettering* in 1918. The top row of *A*s are German Gothic forms from the 1400s through the 1700s. The second row of *A*s are German/Italian Lombardic forms from the 1500s.

Egyptian Hieratic 25th C. B.C.	Semitic Phœnician 10th C. B.C.	Hellenic Early Greek 5th C. B.C.	Roman Early Latin 250 A.D.	Modern Serif 20th C.

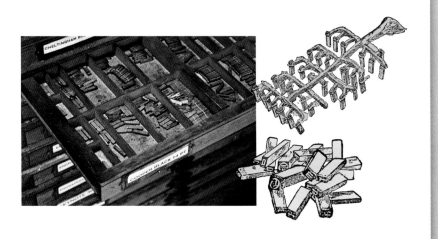

Type was invented in about 1450. Until then, all letter-forms had been handwritten or "script." Johannes Gutenberg figured out how to make bits of metal, each with a raised ink-carrying face, fit together in lines. Hand-set type was such a good technology that it served as the standard for the next 400 years, gradually being replaced by quicker machine set lines of metal type in the later nineteenth and first half of the twentieth centuries.

A font is a set of reproducible characters or "glyphs" that share design attributes. Historically, a font was a metal typeface in a single size, weight, and posture, like 14-point Cooper Black. Changing size, weight, or posture to, say, 18-point Cooper Black, required an entirely different set of metal bits. Each metal font was designed with slightly adjusted proportions to look best at that size.

Introduced in the early 1960s, phototype used a single spinning master negative that could set different sizes of type through a lens. This nullified the optimization of type size proportions, a regrettable condition that has been continued in digital type.

Why does this history matter to a logo designer? Because a logo, above all else, is supposed to be a *distinctive* mark. A logo is a badge of authenticity and requires character. Digital fonts, though, are essentially frozen vegetables: convenient as all get out and adequate for many uses, but not particularly tasty for special projects like logo design without customizing treatments.

A chef takes pride in using fresh ingredients, not frozen ones. The same goes for the logo designer: make your own letterforms (or at least significantly adjust found ones) to produce a character-filled mark.

implse

MEDIAVIEWERS
WWW.IMPLSE.COM

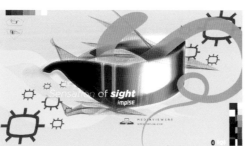

When mixing typefaces, too similar is as bad as too different: either can be mistaken for an accidental design decision. Mixed types shouldn't fight with each other. They should be complementary by sharing shape, proportion, or size. In short, there must be something that is recognizably *right* about the choices.

Start by choosing the letter-form style of the mark's primary type, then narrow choices for the secondary type, as shown on the left in this example. Legibility, especially in the primary type, is much less important than unique character.

MEDIAVIEWERS
WWW.IMPLSE.COM

Good branding requires a typeface that has personality and is different than its competitors'. The best ways to achieve this are to either draw your own letters or significantly alter existing typeface characters.

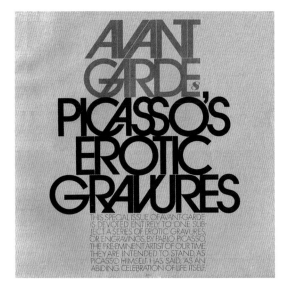

A logo can be expanded into a complete typeface. Avant Garde by Herb Lubalin was one of the first. Lubalin designed interlocking characters (ligatures) for the logo of a new arts magazine. He then expanded the few characters into a full font. The original typeface conversion had many more letter pairs than are included in today's Avant Garde fonts, which kind of negates the idea that made Avant Garde a noteworthy typeface to begin with.

A more recent example is the expansion of the Japanese Glico mark into an entire typeface. Because it is a rather bold, stylized script, this can be more satisfactorily used at larger display sizes than as running text. Still, building a brand — the *consistent experience* of a company — via a proprietary typographic "voice" cannot be argued against.

Type Alteration

Changing type with spatial abstraction is the best way to convert found letterforms — frozen vegetables — into fresh ingredients. ❧ News Gothic, a simple, clean, malleable typeface if ever there was one, can be processed into a new form following distortion, overlapping, and filling in for two variations.

Here are all the logos that appear in a single issue of a newstand magazine. They are shown in relative size to each other as printed. Note that they're almost entirely type-set figures on background. ❧ Which of these is the most distinctive? Which is the most descriptive, the most appealing, the most memorable? If "None of the above" comes to mind, you are becoming sensitive to the realities of logo design.

KÄRNTEN Carinthia

✗ **Bad** Trade Gothic digitally compressed 73%

KÄRNTEN Carinthia

✓ **Good** Trade Gothic Condensed

KÄRNTEN Carinthia

✓ **Good** Trade Gothic

KÄRNTEN Carinthia

✓ **Good** Trade Gothic Extended

KÄRNTEN Carinthia

✗ **Bad** Trade Gothic digitally expanded 140%

One kind of typographic abstraction that must be avoided is digitally expanding and condensing letterforms. The vertical strokes become too thin or too fat, subtly deforming the letters. Many typefaces have a condensed version, and some have an expanded version. Both will have been redrawn to correctly balance vertical and horizontal strokes. Digital contraction and expansion of type is a dead giveaway that the designer is not a *typographer*.

Ship of State

AREPA AЯERA
VENEZUELAN AREPERA & COFFEE SHOP

Here are ideas and examples of type and space abstraction that define and reveal a company's *character*. Each of these ideas is infinitely interpretable, so discern the *idea* rather than its *illustrated expression* to avoid stealing another designer's idea.

➲ Adjust serifs and spacing to create unique kerning pairs.

➲ Wrong reading.

➲ Upside down, here showing the cultural affect of living in the southern hemisphere.

➲ Type size contrast as in this sign in Helsinki and Pompeiian writing prior to 79 AD.

➲ Manipulate the negative space: letters acting as *crema* on a latte — sweet! The simplest letterforms are the most useful for abstraction, and Trade Gothic is an ideal face in this regard. This mark for an upscale hotel restaurant is a wink to those who recognize the reference.

➲ Reverse *some* of the letters, as in this study for a European newspaper.

➲ Exaggerate ascenders or descenders.

➲ Exaggerate *parts* of a letterform — the cross arm of an "E," the serifs of another "E," the circularity of an "O," the curves of an "S."

➲ Draw letters for consistent stroke width to achieve design unity.

➲ Embed secondary type directly into primary letterforms, as in this magazine "flag."

○ Draw it by hand — because no one draws precisely like you! Understand that character-filled calligraphy does not need to be perfect. Messy and distinctive hand lettering can be wonderful.

○ Three-dimensional type can be achieved on computer or off computer.
○ Be noticeably and intentionally playful with color.

- Photo actual letterforms (these were photographed above a Finnish restaurant) and high contrast to black and white.
- Lastly, put the art treatment into the type. Because the image takes the shape of the letters, the letterforms are dominating the image, so they are at the edges of type and space marks.

In type and space logos, as in all marks, *character* is far more important than *legibility*. The top mark reads "Southport" and the bottom mark — a tattoo — has three words and reads *lieben leiden leben*, meaning *"love suffer life"* in German. ❀ Rethink every design's "ought to" and "should" to emphasize originality. Every client deserves a mark they can truly own, as shown here.

The first priority for a message is to *be seen*. Then it can *perhaps* be read and acted on. Messages that are visually indistinct won't be noticed, won't be absorbed, and simply can't be effective.

Express
your ideas
in their
most extreme
form.

Chapter 6

All logos take time and repeat exposure to be recognized and remembered by their audiences. Reading words and letters helps, so an all-image mark is a bigger challenge to achieve its purpose as a key identifier.

In this chapter we'll look at four aspects of the image and space mark (*clockwise from top left*):

Anatomy of an Image and Space Mark and the parts that can be used to build one.

The Figure (Image)/Ground Relationship and how to make them interchangeable.

Semiotics: Icons and Symbols, with the six most useful semiotic categories of signs.

Image-to-Image Relationships and how they introduce dominance and hierarchy.

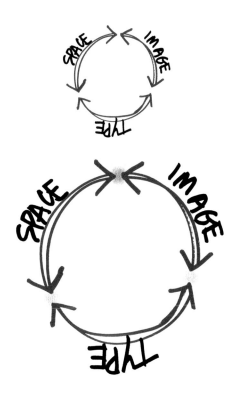

All of design uses just three elements: type, image, and space. Design comes to life when you explore and resolve the overlap between these three elements. In this case, we are concerned with the overlap of image and space: where image becomes space and space becomes image.

Where do image-and-space logos fit into the family of marks? For one thing, an image-and-space *logo* is a terrible misnomer: a "logo" is properly and only a mark that is a pronounceable word, like *Protocoin* or *Farcical Village Plays*. Shown here are *logos*, also called *wordmarks*.

Other marks are all type and space but cannot be read. These are **lettermarks** (sometimes called **monograms**) — type that cannot be read or pronounced.

Some marks are all image and space — no type. These are symbols, of which there are three varieties. There are **arbitrary marks**, which are nonrepresentational and highly abstract (incidentally I have stripped away the color to reveal the ideas more clearly).

No. 5

There are **pictograms**, which are illustrative symbols and somewhat more specific and suggestive but still leave out some details.

There are flat out **representational images** that describe and show precisely what they are. These marks need to be updated whenever the product they represent changes, which introduces continuity problems that only repetition and a large investment of marketing dollars can overcome.

In addition to those three varieties of all-image marks, there are **combination marks**, which include type, image, and space, or in other words, *a symbol joined with either a lettermark or a wordmark.*

Image-and-space marks almost always have some descriptive type or the company's name nearby. This is especially important for smaller companies whose mark isn't being bombarded in front of its audience and must be recognized after only a few impressions. Type acts as a caption with a symbol: it helps viewers *know what they are supposed to think* about the mark.

The Anatomy of an Image and Space Mark

What are the parts that we use in all marks? Fundamentally, we use two: image or "form," which comes in an infinite variety of styles, and space or "counterform," which comes in only two varieties: *background* (the typical kind of space) on the left and *foreground* (the uncommon kind of space) on the right.

Let's look at the transformation of images to create a symbol. What does a designer add to the creation of a logo? Sometimes it is as simple as making the right choice — having good taste.

Sometimes designers need to discern what clients *really* need rather than what they *say* or *think* they need. But ordinarily, the designer is responsible for taking a reasonably straightforward idea — a simple idea, because that is the kind that connects most effectively with an audience — and giving it a characteristic twist to make it the client's own. That requires *translation* or *processing* of visual material.

The Figure (Image)/ Ground Relationship
This is the most basic relationship in design. To ignore ground is to relinquish control over half the terrain of a design. This is particularly important in logo design where there are so few ingredients to work with. Awareness of figure and ground is artistry and craft — and its management is what separates *excellent* design from *ordinary* design.

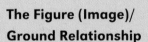

Make the figure and ground ambiguous and interchangeable by specifically making the ground an equally considered shape. Use scale, abstraction, and interaction with the framal reference (or edges of the picture) to create tension between the recognizable figure and the space that surrounds it.

This image shows five birds flying above another bird that is looking up. Though they are all the same scale, the bottom bird is the focal point because it is separated from the group and is the only one not flying. This is a study with six black shapes in front of white space, which if I weren't bringing it up right now, you probably wouldn't notice at all. 🦃 On the right is the same image inverted: not much difference in noticing the now-black counterform.

Here is an extract — a close up — from the previous composition. Notice how the central flying bird is now the focal point: it is the only one not bleeding off the edges of the composition.

Changing the scale of one bird changes the perspective to a *worm's eye view*. This is an entirely different interaction between the focal point and the gang of flying birds: less background space; the space that exists connects; more "sticking your beak into other birds' business."

Now there are fewer birds. How few can there be and still tell the story? It is always good to remove unnecessary elements for simplicity's sake. The only way to know what's necessary is to experiment with multiple studies. The emphasis has been changed again, now to the flying birds' perspective. Scale changes our perception of space. ❧ On the right is the same image inverted.

Now there are even fewer birds: just two, which is the minimum necessary to express a relationship, and there is less of each of them: one is just the head and beak, and neither shows wings, so these are now *highly abstracted birds*. Take every idea to its most extreme interpretation so you can retreat to an iteration that is most satisfying. ❧ On the right is the same image inverted. The vast space between the birds is undeniably present. But this version seems a bit *arbitrary*.

Finally, with multiple experiments to familiarize ourselves with the material at hand, a relationship emerges, a *correspondence* is found, between the upraised beak and the gap just in front of the hawk's tail. The alignment of similar shapes makes this a more *purposeful* and more satisfying design, and the background shape has been activated as a full partner in the composition.

Attend to the space in a design, and the figures will seem to magically take care of themselves. Attend only to the figures, and the design is much more likely to fail — and by that I mean it will be merely mediocre. I have deconstructed a mark for a concert promoter by Australian designer Warren Taylor. Here is a collection of musical instruments, rendered as silhouettes.

Now here is the same artwork showing the spaces between the instruments. This is "active" ground, so called because it is nearest the figures and thus most noticeable when it is changed.

Cattleyard

By changing the negative spaces — but not the musical instrument "positive" shapes — we have crafted an entirely different design. Replace the positive shapes to reveal a cow made of musical instruments. Add the type and you have a mark that represents the organization's nickname, "Groovin' the Moo."

The mark on the left is a charming line drawing and type in front of background. It is purely figure in front of ground. The mark on the right, for a chef's club, has activated space: the DKR letters are actually background (the black shape surrounds white space that we see as letterforms), and the skull between the two rats is made from the interior form of the animals and the careful positioning of kitchen utensils.

Here is a compilation of many of the marks used in this chapter shown in grayscale to simplify their figure/ground qualities. Some have more compelling ground manipulation. Can you identify them?

They are grouped "above the line." Ask yourself, *as a group*, are they more effective logos and marks than the marks and logos "below the line," those that do not use space as vigorously? In *my* opinion, there is no question that they are decidedly more effective.

Semiotics: Icons and Symbols

Before getting into the somewhat more complicated subject of semiotics, it is useful to discuss icons and symbols. What is the difference between an icon and a symbol? According to the dictionary, an **icon** (from the Greek for *likeness* or *image*) is an image, picture, representation, likeness, symbol, or sign — or "a graphic representation on a video display terminal."

The definition of **symbol** is a shape or sign used to represent something; a sign, image, metaphor, icon, ideogram, mark, logo, or emblem. The two terms then are, in general, interchangeable.

Symbols and icons are typically categorized by their level of abstraction, of which there are three. However, I must say that declaring "three levels of abstraction" and having marks find their *one* category to drop into, like coins rolling down the ramp in a plastic bank, is too simple. The demarcations between the three categories of symbols overlap, so some flexibility of thinking is needed.

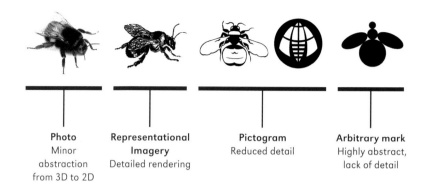

Photo
Minor abstraction from 3D to 2D

Representational Imagery
Detailed rendering

Pictogram
Reduced detail

Arbitrary mark
Highly abstract, lack of detail

These are the three levels of abstraction:

Representational images show precisely what they are and are the lowest level of abstraction.

Pictograms are illustrative symbols that are less abstract than arbitrary marks but still leave out some details. They can be used to describe an idea.

Arbitrary marks are nonrepresentational, highly abstract images and are the highest level of abstraction.

Rebus puzzles have been around since the Egyptians. The idea of a rebus (from Latin meaning "by things"; *non verbis sed rebus*: "not by words but by things") is that images can be interpreted purely on the sound they make when spoken, not on their inherent meaning. At top are coasters from Narragansett brewery and designer Adam Aud which are fun to decipher over a cold beverage. Below are five historical examples.

Now, on to the subject of **semiotics**, which is the study of language and signs, their meanings, and *how their meanings are understood.* There are three branches of semiotics: **semantics**, the relation of signs to the things they represent; **syntactics**, the relation of signs to each other and the rules that govern how they combine to make phrases and sentences; and **pragmatics**, the relation of signs to the context in which they are used.

SEMIOTICS

Semantics

The relation of signs and words to the things they represent: what does a sign mean? (for example, red means stop, danger, hot); can the sign be misunderstood?

Syntactics

The relation of language and signs to each other; the rules that govern how signs combine to make phrases and sentences; parts of a sign joined together; whether a sign is part of a system of related signs.

Pragmatics

The relation of signs and language to the context in which they are used (as when a diplomat says yes, he means 'perhaps'; when he says perhaps, he means 'no'; and when he says no, he is not a diplomat); how context affects meaning.

Ferdinand de Saussure (1857–1913) is considered the father of modern linguists. One of his ideas is that no word or symbol is *inherently* meaningful. It is only a **signifier** (a representation of something) that must be combined in the brain with the **signified** (an idea of the thing itself) in order to be given meaning as a "sign." In this way, all signs are merely *hints*, and that is key to giving a visual reminder of a branding *experience*, which is what a logo should do.

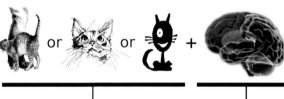

Signifier	Brain	Signified
A representation of something	Mixing bowl	*Idea* of object

or — or — + — + — *Idea* of object

Representational Signs
Realistic images of objects

Ideograms
Nonrepresentational ideas

Pictograms
Descriptive images of objects

Synonymic Signs
Images representing the same object or idea

Symbolic Signs
Pictograms with new meanings

Arbitrary Signs
Nonrepresentational, random

I have simplified semiotics' varieties of signs into the six most eloquent and distinct categories. The simplest to recognize is the representational sign, because it shows pretty much just what it is: it is a realistic picture of an object. But even this simplest category is a bit complicated because any sign, even a simple sign, can be interpreted a few ways.

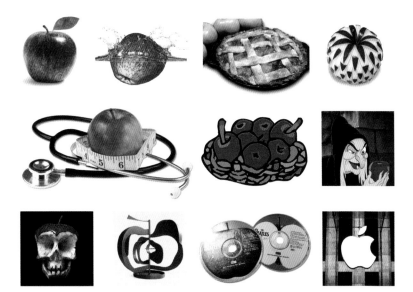

A picture of an apple can indicate a *kind of apple*, like a Red Delicious (semantics); or it can be a sign for *food and sustenance*; or it can be a sign for *healthy living and doctor avoidance in general*; or it can be a sign for *poison or biblical temptation*; or it can be a sign for a well-known computer company (syntactics). It all depends, often on the context in which the sign is perceived (pragmatics).

In descending order of abstraction, these are the six most useful categories of signs:

Representational sign

Realistic image of an object: you can tell what kind of bird it is. Make this from a photograph or use a picture font or, better, select from collections of EPS files. These are from Ultimate Symbols' *Nature Icons*.

Representational Signs
Realistic images of objects

This mark shows a realistic interpretation (*bottom left*) of the Rainerhof, a historic building in the main square of Klagenfurt, Austria, that sits behind the renowned Lindwurm, the dragon statue that has been part of the city's coat of arms since 1583 (*upper right*). These two shapes are at once descriptive, simplified, and scaled, ensuring they relate into a single mark.

RAINERHOF

RAINERHOF

Pictograms
Descriptive images of objects

Pictogram Descriptive image of object: you can tell it is a bird, but not necessarily what kind of bird. Less detail than representational sign. Road signs, airport signs, and clothing laundering tags use pictograms because they are universally understood. Pictograms predate alphabetic writing and evolved simultaneously in present-day Syria and ancient China. Pictograms, early written marks, represented objects while ideograms represented ideas.

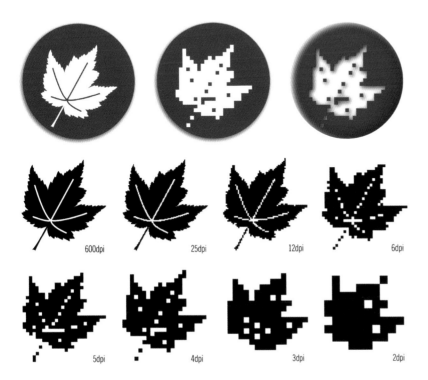

600dpi · 25dpi · 12dpi · 6dpi
5dpi · 4dpi · 3dpi · 2dpi

Abstraction of imagery is the key ingredient in converting a representational sign into a pictogram, or a broader symbol of an idea. This can also be important in establishing differentiation from similar marks. Pixilation, shown here, is similar to a photographic "test strip" that expresses steps in value and contrast, but this works with steps in resolution. A realistic leaf becomes a symbol of a leaf simply by removing detail.

Symbolic sign A pictogram with an additional or alternate meaning. This new meaning has to be learned, as an arrow through a heart meaning "love" or a light bulb meaning "idea." As writing evolved, marks developed from drawings of objects (pictograms) to increasingly abstract marks (symbolic signs, ideograms, and alphabets) as the need for more complex communication progressed.

The leaf shape and green color symbolize ecology; the arrow symbolizes "active," motion, and process; and the dimensionality shows "real" or "authentic." The leaf is centered over neither the full name, the word "actively," nor the i to show motion. The type choice is a humanist sans serif which implies "not machine made." ❋ Paul Rand's 1944 mark for the Helbros Watch Company is a distinctive lowercase "H," but it symbolizes the mainspring of a mechanical watch.

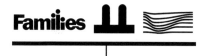

Symbolic Signs
Pictograms with new meanings

Ideograms
Nonrepresentational ideas

| Powder | Small particle | Large particle | Emulsion | Soluble powder |

Ideogram Nonrepresentational image of an idea. An ideogram differs from a symbolic sign in that is it is an *arbitrary* mark. It represents an *idea* or an *action*, or an object that is *conceptual* rather than actual. Like symbolic signs, the meaning of ideograms must be learned. The ideograms in the bottom row are used in the agricultural industry. Separated from their meaning, they can be used for their simple and elegant form alone.

This ideogram mark is an extension built on an abstract rendering of the letter "N." Rather than representing any particular flower, this organic mark symbolizes *growth* and *nature*. Designer Lu Feng relates artwork and type by inserting the center of the artwork in grayscale into the type. The grayscale contrast has been reduced to emphasize the legibility of the characters.

Synonymic sign A synonym is a word that means the same or nearly the same as another word, like *machine* and *contraption*. Synonymic signs are likewise images with the same referent. It is essential to develop a distinctive rendition of a synonymic sign so it can be distinguished from similar marks for the referent.

Synonymic Signs
Images representing the same object or idea

Arbitrary mark Nonrepresentational, highly abstract image; the highest level of abstraction. Arbitrary marks are useful for companies that do many things and cannot be shown with greater specificity. ✾ Understanding signs and their categories empowers you to explore each one intentionally and *choose* the amount of abstraction that is appropriate for your client.

Arbitrary Signs
Nonrepresentational, random

Image-to-Image Relationships

The last section of this chapter is about creating interesting and unexpected image-to-image (with space) relationships. This should be every bit as much conscious design decisions as choosing lettering styles or colors.

The first thing to decide is whether and how much to make the images similar. *Shape or size similarity*, for example, ensure design unity, even if the two images are conceptually quite different from each other.

If you opt for *dissimilarity*, the question is how much contrast to use and in what ways. Here is a basic chart of contrasts that will get you well on your way to trying a variety of new approaches. We will try them on the birds artwork.

CONTRASTS

Space	Position	Form
Filled : Empty	Above : Below	Simple : Complex
Active : Passive	Left : Right	Realistic : Abstract
Near : Distant	Isolated : Grouped	Organic : Geometric
2D : 3D	Centered : Asymmetrical	Rectilinear : Curvilinear

Direction	Texture	Density
Horizontal : Vertical	Rough : Smooth	Thick : Thin
Forward : Backward	Reflective : Matte	Solid : Liquid
Stable : Moving	Sticky : Slippery	Liquid : Gas
Converging : Diverging	Fuzzy : Bald	Opaque : Transparent

Size	Color	Gravity
Big : Little	Grays : Color	Heavy : Light
Wide : Narrow	Warm : Cool	Stable : Unstable
Expanded : Condensed	Bright : Dull	Grounded : Floating
Deep : Shallow	Saturated : Neutral	Serious : Superficial

Space contrast

2D : 3D. I have inserted a photo of a mosaic of a fish, which contrasts with the flat area of color.

Position contrast
Isolated : Grouped. Lone wolf against an army of pigeons?

Form contrast
Organic : Geometric. Maximum contrast looks intentional, so go *really* fuzzy and *really* geometric.

Direction contrast

Stable : Moving. I used a few Photoshop tips and tricks to smear the flying bird and bring it back to line art.

Texture contrast

Rough : Smooth. The lower bird has been filled with a detail from a block print of a Southwestern motif.

Density contrast
Liquid : gas. I have inserted high contrast photos of clouds and seawater into the birds.

Size contrast
Big : Little. Bigger is perceived as nearer, so our view appears to have gotten lower to the ground.

Color contrast

Warm : cool. Warm colors appear closer and cool colors recede, so anything meant to look "in front" or "nearer" should be a warm color. Overlapping elements furthers the illusion. Remember: color is relative — every color is only warm or cool in *comparison* to another color.

Gravity contrast

Heavy : light. This was trickier than the others, but ended up rather well.

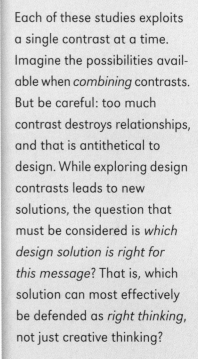

Each of these studies exploits a single contrast at a time. Imagine the possibilities available when *combining* contrasts. But be careful: too much contrast destroys relationships, and that is antithetical to design. While exploring design contrasts leads to new solutions, the question that must be considered is *which design solution is right for this message*? That is, which solution can most effectively be defended as *right thinking*, not just creative thinking?

As with all design, you can get away with anything you can dream up if *it looks like it was done intentionally*. Figuring out how to make our design decisions *look intentional* is the path designers follow, and it is the challenge that keeps design fascinating.

Draw as many thumbnails as you can dream up. Do at least a dozen *different* ideas a day for as many days as you have. One idea will lead to another. Only at the end, launch into the editing process.

Design uses
divergent thinking
*to generate
many ideas and*
convergent thinking
*to combine the best
into final studies.*

How to
Type, Image, and Space
Build a Logo

Chapter 7

In previous chapters we have looked at how a logo fits into a branding effort; how a type-and-space logo is put together; and how an image-and-space mark works.

Now it's time to bring all the pieces together and look at how type, image, and space coexist in a unified mark. We will look at how image and type work together — as opposed to merely being *near* one another — and then we'll add space on top of that pairing to see how all three elements can be distilled into a singular, descriptive, potent mark.

Image, type, and space are the three elements designers have to work with. These elements are inherently different from one another. Making them look like they belong together — by manipulating them in the areas where one *can* be perceived as another — is the designer's challenge. It is irrefutable evidence that a designer has achieved a superior solution.

Having "nothing wrong" with a design is a very poor second place to having "something right" with a design. So in logo design, it is easy to have three different elements — image, type, and space — remain looking different: anyone can do that. But it is much harder to cook them into an alloy in which the constituent parts become better in the presence of the others. These logo updates as described in the *New York Times* show a trend toward less authoritarian marks.

There are eight combinations of emphases in which image, type, and space can interact, two of which are equivalent (and not especially useful, because they are both equally weighted and if everything in a design is *equally* noisy or *equally* subdued, nothing stands out). But there are an infinite — or near infinite — number of ways of executing interpretations of these relationships. Getting a grip on the limited range of approaches leads to expressive solutions. Being compulsive or thorough in trying each relationship will uncover solutions that would remain unconsidered otherwise. The alternative to a thorough effort is thrusts in the dark, with a hoped-for "good idea" happening to get skewered on your computer.

IMAGETYPESPACE
IMAGETYPESPACE
IMAGETYPE**SPACE**
IMAGETYPESPACE
IMAGETYPESPACE
IMAGE**TYPE**SPACE
IMAGETYPE**SPACE**
IMAGE**TYPESPACE**

This client had a list of preferences based on history and likes that led to two solutions: one that emphasized *location*, the other that emphasized *activity*. Their history showed examples of both these directions.

The only location for the client's logo would be as a vehicle sticker (an oval preferred), and the two most popular vehicle colors among the client's members are white and black, so the mark would need to be legible at a particular scale and against two particular colors. These preliminary studies didn't satisfy because they "were not fishy enough."

Fish seemed to be essential as content, but identifying any *particular* fish would be problematic: the members know their fish, so choosing as fine a detail as a particular fish's face or fin would show favoritism. So fish *symbolism* was the right choice. 🐟 Fish scales are much more abstract than fish faces as a fundamental fishy attribute. But the members also know their fish scales, so no particular scales could be used.

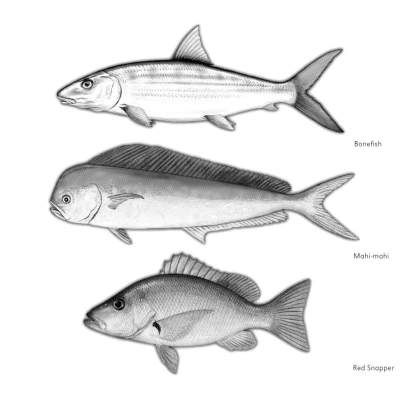

Bonefish

Mahi-mahi

Red Snapper

Because fish scales are smooth, they are hard to photograph as *texture*. The best representations are drawn, which wasn't wanted. So the designer stepped outside that hopeless tar pit of conflict and chose *feathers* for the fish scale texture. Specifically, a suitably abstracted ultra-close-up of a bird's wing feathers. Given the issues around choosing particular fish scales, the ends can justify the means.

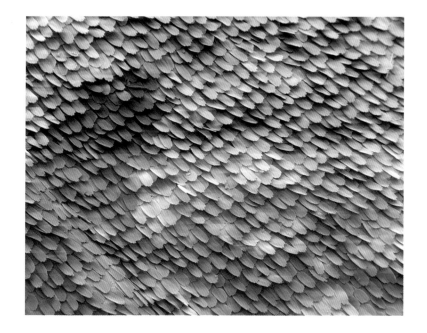

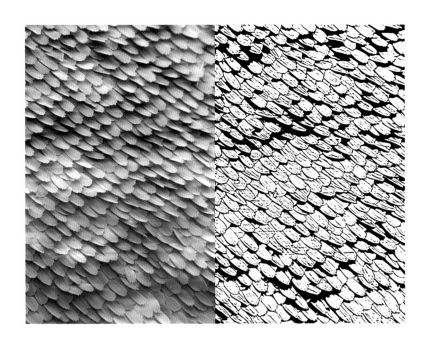

Converted to high contrast, it communicates surface texture well. And the scale, the *size of detail*, disguises the actual source of the texture. (To date, not one member has asked about which precise "fish" is being represented.) It also happens to look a bit like water, which is appropriate and can be exploited.

The map is much easier: any reasonably accurate map of the tip of Florida showing the group's territory from Lake Okeechobee to the end of the Keys would suffice. The designer used a tourist brochure's map and traced over it in Illustrator, creating an easily recognizable, high-contrast silhouette of the region. The Keys were enlarged to be sure they could be seen on the final.

Treating the image of flats fisherpersons, supplied by the client, needed to be handled in a fashion similar to the map for consistency and for comparison: a black silhouette of figures on a specialized boat. Passion must be taken seriously: club members can actually identify *the engine make* from this crude artwork.

So now we have all the parts. Aside from their shared contrast, they haven't much visually to do with one another yet: they do not have *inherent* design unity. Here's how they were put together.

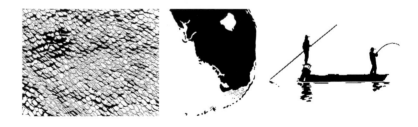

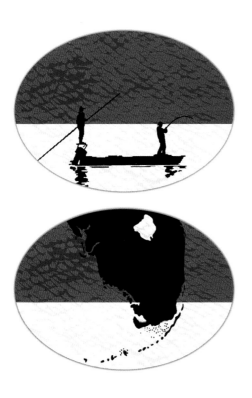

First, just the images. The feathers/scales were tinted into deep red and light gray to ghost over the white and red sunset background, implying water surface and clouds in one, and northern and southern regions of water in the map. The fishing figures and map were silhouetted in black in the foreground.

A first pass at adding type (that's a typeface called Bello Small Caps) is added in the least valuable areas. The type is placed on the horizon behind the fishermen, making them more dimensional, and there is some careful letterspacing going on behind the pole to optimize legibility of the word "Florida." Similarly, the dot has been placed in a relationship with the "hooked up" fisherman, unifying type and image.

The final pass at adding type replaces Bello *Small Caps* with Bello *Script* in the primary instance, which seemed more Floridian and appropriate. It also can be tweaked to fit the top-half space better and contrasts with the redundant website address.

This is the final that was selected, the two previous identifiers, and the four parts from which it was made.

sixthsense

Here is a handsome mark that has much to recommend it. The tight letterspacing makes the name a wordmark rather than mere typesetting. Even as nice a design as this may have some design relationships that could be made clearer. The primary colors are blue and orange. Why is the image in gray and orange?

sixthsense

sixthsense

The explorations take advantage of existing attributes and maximize them. An evolutionary process, each step is taken as a consequence of the previous change. What if we unify the design by changing gray to the blue in the name? It is now a *little* simpler, a *little* more unified. 🖌 Next, replace the dot's color over the "i" with the orange of "sense" and reverse the colors in the art. This is a step back: "sixth" and the hand with the six relate and should both be blue.

Now, why is the art the *exact* size it is? There doesn't appear to be any connectedness with the other elements — it is a pleasant size, certainly, but it isn't a clear, clean relationship. Let's look at some alternative size relationships that will perhaps be clearer. ❀ Match the art's width to the width of "sixth" and align it over that emphasized word.

Match the art's width to the width of "sense," and align it over the emphasized word. This is nearly the same width as the previous study. Reduce space between the bottom of the art so it aligns with the top of the h's ascender.

sixthsense

Match the art's width to the overall width of the type. The relative proportions are now completely rebalanced with an overwhelming emphasis on the imagery. This may not make it a suitable mark.

sixthsense

sixthsense

sixthsense

sixthsense

sixthsense

sixthsense

These six studies use precisely the same elements and offer a palette of good choices that have a range of visible relationships that make a client's company look attentive and well run. Some solutions are "better" than others, but these all have a justifiable reason for looking as they do — they are not random solutions based on "liking." Using logic to solve a visual problem adds a degree of rightness to a design and *that's* clothing a company properly.

Now let's use a flamboyantly colorful and active illustration to explore the four ways type, image, and space can interact in a mark:

ONE Elements can be near each other

TWO Elements can be aligned with each other

THREE Elements can have shared attributes

FOUR Elements are secondary to activated white space

ONE Elements can be **near each other** but not in any discernible relationship other than their proximity. This is the weakest pseudo-relationship. Basically, the only thing they have in common is proximity. They don't share form or color or texture or alignment. Finding examples of this category is easy: these are logos in which there is nothing wrong, yet there is nothing particularly *right* with them, either.

Oh Boy!

Art Stylists is a Spanish hair salon, which explains the hairy grass across the bottom. The strokes of these Helvetica Light letterforms could be similarly treated for greater unity. The asymmetry (space adds quality and sensitivity to artistic principles) and period at the end of the name — giving it forceful emphasis — both add significant character.

The "Plum" is a delight with it's green-leaf ear. But "organics" is random (or default: it's Helvetica again): it could be bigger or it could be smaller, and it could be another typeface entirely. In short, what is right with "organics"?

This is charmingly drawn art, and the mark has thoughtful type adjustment into an organic-looking ligature. The art and type have greenness and *proximity* in common, but is that enough? The slices of white in the "SO" ligature is very open, echoing the words' letterspacing and ensuring the ligature doesn't become too thick and dark in comparison. Is the "l" optically centered between the "p" and the "y"?

This leaf is a wonderful expression that the client can own. And relating the art to type via color is a terrific start. But the art and letterforms don't share much else in common (the thick/thin in the wavy lines of the art?), and using a second typeface for "MUSIC" is unnecessary.

a s p a r a g u s

The art and letterforms (the typeface is Birch Standard) in this mark for a French/Vietnamese restaurant don't share form so they don't appear to belong together. Of the two, the art is much more distinctive, so the letterforms should be chosen to echo some aspect of the art. The geometric curves would be the best place to start. Perhaps the French spelling would have been too foreign: *asperge*, with the asparagus around the central "e."

Oh Boy!

TWO Elements can be aligned with each other. Here they share width.

Here their alignment is even more pronounced. By chopping off pieces, background space comes to the front.

Alignment can occur where the elements agree on any of the four perimeter edges or on a clearly visible *internal* spine. There doesn't have to be any more relationship than one of *position*. In my opinion, this is the minimal relationship that must be achieved to make a logo look intentionally designed.

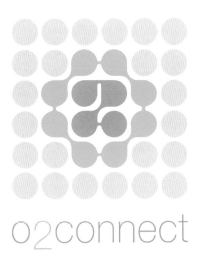

o2connect

This artwork is delicious! Look at that central number "2." The gooey joiners in the green and orange dots indicate people-to-people connected-ness. The color use is unifying, and the type is set to match the width of the art. Note that the color of the "2" has been reversed in the type below.

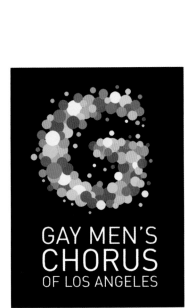

GAY MEN'S
CHORUS
OF LOS ANGELES

Width is the common denomi-nator in this handsome mark that uses meaningful rainbow colors and less meaningful yet inescapable references to the color-blindness studies conducted by Dr. Shinobu Ishihara in 1917.

The art is vertically aligned over the half-filled "O," suggesting a *process*, maybe evaporation. This is a fine example of integrating image and type into a unified mark.

Alignment can also be found in the continuation of a line, as in the angle from the top of the stroke of the "y" and the beginning of the "road" that crosses the book. This mark is for an online story and picture-sharing site.

In order to align the five dots in this mark, the letterforms had to be drawn from scratch. It is clear the dots are intended to be dominant over the letters because the "P" had to be made overly tall and the middle dot in the "P" exceeds its vertical stroke, an unusual feature in most renditions of the letter.

bike & walk marlborough

The width of the three lines of type match the width of the "M" (for Marlborough?) within the green oval. The combination of feet and bicycle chain is a convincing merging of disparate images. Reducing the size of the ampersand to the x-height of "bike" also reduces its width, which looks odd. That is, its being green makes it look like it belongs to the "M" art more than its surrounding type.

The addition of a single, ordinary vertical stroke positioned precisely — and the use of light and bold weights of Interstate typeface — implies action with elegance.

FREEZE|FRAME

Flush-left type agrees with the central axis of the artwork. Overlapped silhouettes express a specific location (the dome of Vietri sul Mare's Church of San Giovanni Battista) and subject (classical music represented by a violin). The violin's "f" hole doubles as a letterform, though it looks too far away from the rest of the word "estival."

The
Amalfi
Coast
Music
f estival
& Institute™

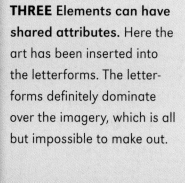

THREE Elements can have shared attributes. Here the art has been inserted into the letterforms. The letter-forms definitely dominate over the imagery, which is all but impossible to make out.

Here the shared attributes — the art and "Oh Boy!" — are overlapping so the row of plus signs now look separated from the joined primary combination mark.

A shared attribute can be where one element forces itself into or onto the other. This is leaps and bounds ahead of alignment, because *all* the other attributes a form can have are considered and can be transferred or applied to the other elements.

Shared color is the strongest relationship between this art and type, though the stroke weight of "greenhouse" also matches the flask. "Greenhouse" is optically centered vertically between the art and the secondary type (the two negative spaces are equalized). The tagline is sized to be the width of "reenhouse," aligning to the right of the descender of the "g."

greenhouse™
organic content management.

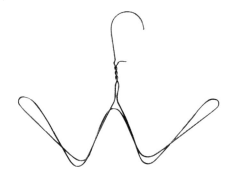

fashionworks

The shared stroke width of the image and the letterforms unifies this mark. The hanger has been bent to reveal an "f" and a "w." The Futura Light "f" of the typeset word has been adjusted to be more curved at the top, echoing the hanger's shape. If "fashionworks" had been sized or spaced to equal the width of the hanger, it would have been a more intentional decision.

KoMunity
PROJECT

The thick-thin weight of the four characters in the art is approximated in the hand-lettered name. The spacing attributes are equivalent, too, and that is hard to achieve. To funk up the work so it resonates with its intended youngish audience (QuickSilver Clothing sponsored this outreach program), intentional misspelling is used, as is a graffito-like "un" ligature. Now, what is right with the typeset "PROJECT"?

The distinctive letterforms and position of the "c" initial are based on the shape of the hole in a can. When a design solution appears obvious as is this one, the details of its execution like precise spacing attributes become conspicuous.

Wiggly, sloppy, spilled, *handmade-esque* (but not actually hand drawn!) letters and rough coffee beans and cup in coffee-brown make a very personable mark. Note that this is a font that has been overlaid with two drawn coffee beans. The giveaway that it is a font rather than original calligraphy are the twin "s" and "f" — their outlines should have been tweaked to change one of each so they looked hand drawn.

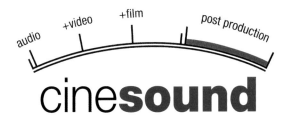

Using art and type that references industry standards and colors to explain the direct link of *sound* to *postproduction* in this tasty and utterly defendable solution. Refreshing not to see sound waves (da-na-na-na-na-na-na) used for a business that works with sound. All type is in the Helvetica family.

The image of splashing water interacts with the letterforms so it becomes hard to recognize where one begins and the other ends. Letters are dominated by imagery over the "A" and "T," and the image is dominated by the letters over the "W," "E," and "R." Contrast is expressed in the organic splash and rigidity of the sans serif letters.

FOUR Elements are secondary to activated white space. Activating white space should be part of every series of logo studies. It is excellent mental exercise and forces fresh thinking. ✺ This is the highest state of logo design, because it is the hardest to achieve. It looks the most intentional, that is, activated white space *always* looks like the least random design solution.

The missing element will almost certainly become the focal point, so choose the most valuable part to get the treatment. This mark shows two letters: "S" and "U." The "S" is created where the two outer shapes end. This German name translates as "Sulz Difference," Sulz being a German city whose perimeter is shown in the map. "GmbH" is the equivalent of the British "Ltd." or American "Inc."

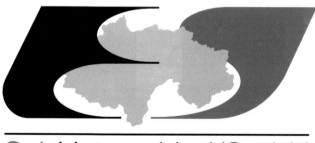

SulzUnterschied/GmbH

This letterform is crafted with delicately sized and positioned quote marks in the counter-spaces — suitable art for a translation service. Because of the infinite variability, such counterspace interpretation continues to be a fruitful area for designers.

Making "milk" look liquid — and spilling into the blue puddle — requires a deft touch, especially where the letters join the perimeter of the pool. This is a soft, inviting mark for a clothing boutique.

The use of imagery as letterspacing is unexpected, deliberate, and distinctive. This limited palette of figures (one in various sizes, always in white) contrasts with the much more expansive color palette.

The counterspaces of letterforms have been used many times as art, but these counters haven't even needed any adjustment to work for a popsicle shop. This is just type with three "sticks."

IMAGETYPESPACE

IMAGETYPESPACE

IMAGETYPE**SPACE**

IMAGETYPESPACE

IMAGETYPESPACE

IMAGE**TYPE**SPACE

IMAGETYPE**SPACE**

IMAGE**TYPESPACE**

So, to recap, there are eight combinations of emphases in which image, type, and space can interact, and each combination will lead to a *different balance* among the elements being used.

sixthsense

sixthsense

sixthsense

sixthsense

sixthsense

sixthsense

By making elements relate in all of the available permutations, a series of equally considered design solutions will be achieved.

There are four ways to relate elements and some are better than others.

ONE Elements can be near each other, which is the weakest relationship.

TWO Elements can be aligned, which is the minimal relationship that must be achieved to make a logo look intentionally designed.

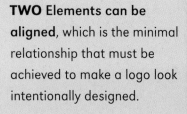

THREE Elements can have **shared attributes** where one element forces itself into or onto the other, and

FOUR Elements are **secondary to activated white space**, which is the highest state of logo design because it is the most *intentional* design solution.

APPENDIX I

10 Mistakes Designers Make When Creating Logos

1. **Not pairing abstraction to the scale of the business** Match the logo with the character and nature of the business. A local plumbing service needs greater specificity than a regional plumbing supply company, and a national plumbing manufacturer can use still more abstraction.

2. **Attending only to figure and neglecting ground** Logos are such fine gems that every part must be considered and fully used.

3. **Designing a logo in a vacuum** Don't design for yourself. Collect competitors' logos and design to exceed that specific universe. Present these logos to the client before showing your own studies to provide context.

4. **Neglecting to blend at least two distinctive ideas together for fresh results** "Barbecue" plus "Iceland" are far more useful together than alone as descriptors of an Icelandic restaurant.

5. **Not basing a design on strategic goals** What is the client's brand position? Your client's pursuit of business success has a strategy. The logo is part of that plan.

6. **Designing without an idea** Write an idea down in words before you begin to give the idea form.

7. **Not investing time to understand the client's unique standing in the business community** What makes them viable and how can those qualities be expressed symbolically?

8. **Using the same pieces as everyone else** Neutral is forgettable. Quirky — in a way that promotes character — is memorable. The fonts and treatments on your computer are like frozen vegetables: mix them any way you like but there is a limit to how distinctive your cooking can be. Instead, craft materials off computer and then import them.

9. **Showing too many versions** You are being paid to be thoughtful: show no more than four or five studies in the first pass. More looks indecisive.

10. **Not preparing scalable artwork that ensures all type and spacing remain consistently the same** Don't give the client an opportunity to alter your design.

APPENDIX II

23 Ways to Generate Visual Ideas

1. Reassess all assumptions, challenge old ideas and preconceptions.
2. Describe the key subject in words. Translate words into visuals.
3. Stratify the data to express hierarchy visually.
4. Step from the specific to a general definition of the subject.
5. Look for patterns in order to create order out of chaos.
6. Define the subject, then reverse it to transform the familiar into the strange.
7. Find an analogy in a different area paralleling this problem.
8. Make connections and look for the unexpected.
9. Substitute a pictorial metaphor for the subject.
10. Define outside influences, relationships, and implications.
11. Use your hands to describe action, purpose, or direction.
12. What is the source of the subject? Where does it come from, what causes it?
13. How is the subject delivered?
14. What direction does it come from?
15. How might another profession react to the problem?
16. How are the involved parties likely to react?
17. What is the subject's scale and emotional relationship to the key message?
18. What is the subject's bulk and density: emotional or physical?
19. What is the subject's value: its basis in human need, the motivation for it?
20. Where is this happening?
21. What is the time of day/weather?
22. Where can it be viewed from?
23. When did it happen in history?

APPENDIX VIIa

Quotations

Thoughtful insights from others

Genius ain't nothing more than elegant common sense. Josh Billings

I can see beauty where others see ugliness. That either makes me an artist, or a person of very poor taste. Anonymous

To invent, you need a good imagination and a pile of junk. Thomas Edison

APPENDIX III

18 Tools for Graphic Surprise

1. **Bright color:** deliberate splash of hue in photo or unusual combinations in art
2. **Powerful mood:** strong emotional image, landscape, or rendered concept
3. **Violent action** movement or blurred photos
4. **Startling size:** use unexpected scale of life-size or larger image
5. **Large type:** blowing up a word or two in huge type
6. **Focus on viewer:** subject jumps off page or looks directly into reader's eyes
7. **Unusual viewpoint:** pictures taken from impossible vantage points
8. **Telling detail** focusing onto a vivid microcosm of the whole
9. **Butting images** in irregular or intermixed shapes
10. **Cubist repetition** within one image showing several versions of the same subject
11. **Repetition over space and time** showing change in the same subject
12. **Dimension contrast** of naturalistic figures on two-dimensional backgrounds or vice versa
13. **Exaggerating the normal;** the one-two punch: normal at first glance, startling afterwards
14. **Twisting the normal:** manipulating the normal a little bit
15. **Incongruity:** surreal, impossible combinations of naturalistic elements
16. **Visual puns:** literal images made to look like something else
17. **Exaggerate the human form**
18. **Animals:** realistic or anthropomorphic?

APPENDIX VIIb

Quotations

Thoughtful insights from others

In marketing you must choose between boredom, shouting and seduction. Which do you want? Roy H. Williams

One need not be aware of technicalities to perceive beauty and order. Paul Epstein (On Bach's "Art of Fugue")

Stare. It is the way to educate your eyes. And more. Stare, pry, listen, eavesdrop. Die knowing something. You are not here long. Walker Evans, photographer.

APPENDIX IV

10 Ways to Encourage Ideation

1. **Keep an open mind.**
2. **Be aware all the time.** Creativity relies on combinations. You never know when inspiration might hit.
3. **Avoid "They'll never buy this"** or "They won't understand this."
4. **Don't hold back.** Be absurd.
5. **Take risks.** Be like Columbus sailing over the edge of the world.
6. **Think of work as fun.** Don't take it too seriously. Stop judging yourself.
7. **Take time to think.** Few ideas are "inspiration." Most come from work.
8. **Develop an annotated file of ideas and refer to it.** Use Post-Its to remember what you found so interesting.
9. **Come back to it later.** The brain works while you are resting.
10. **Take notes all the time.** Ideas evaporate unless you capture them.

APPENDIX VIIc

Quotations

Thoughtful insights from others

The creative act does not create something out of nothing. It uncovers, selects, reshuffles, combines, synthesizes already existing facts, ideas, faculties, skills. Typically, the more familiar the parts, the more striking the new whole. Arthur Koestler

What you see depends to a great extent on what you expect to see, what you are used to. Jonathan Miller

The task of the designer is to give visual access to the subtle and difficult — that is the revelation of the complex. Edward Tufte

Imagination is a muscle you can develop. Luis Buñuel

Through the picture we see reality and through the word we understand it. Through the drawing we understand the photo and through the photo we believe the drawing. Sven Lidman

A great trademark is appropriate, dynamic, distinctive, memorable and unique. Primo Angeli

Don't worry about people stealing your ideas. If your ideas are any good, you'll have to ram them down people's throats. Howard Aiken

You can't depend on your eyes, when your imagination is out of focus. Mark Twain

APPENDIX V

Alex Osborn's Checklist

This is one of the most effective thinking tools used for change, modification, and development. Osborn (1888–1966) was an advertising executive and creativity theorist who invented brainstorming.

Enlarge

What can be made larger, higher, wider, thicker, stronger, heavier, longer, faster, or more frequent?

What can be added, increased, exaggerated, multiplied, or intensified?

What can be given extra value or a plus ingredient?

Reduce

What can be smaller, lower, thinner, weaker, lighter, shorter, slower?

What can be reduced, eliminated, subtracted, or condensed?

What can be miniaturized or streamlined?

Substitute

What or who else we use instead?

Can we use another material, process, energy source, time, or place?

What other ingredients can we use?

What other alternatives are available?

Combine

What can be blended or alloyed?

What units, ideas, services, functions, events, purposes, or facilities can we combine?

Rearrange

What components, parts, or units can be interchanged?

Can we change pace, schedule, sequence, design, pattern, shape, or material?

Reverse

Can elements change roles or positions?

Can we turn it upside down, invert it, or switch outside to inside or front to back?

Modify

Can we modify the purpose, functions, contents, movement, shape, or sound?

What could be given a new twist or new emphasis?

Adapt

What else is like this or what can we copy?

Does the past offer any parallels?

What other ideas does this suggest?

APPENDIX VI

Opposites and Attributes

These will spark new ideas.

Opposites

Weak/Strong	Smooth/Rough
Thin/Thick	Straight/Bent
Hard/Soft	Round/Square
High/Low	Antique/Modern
Dry/Wet	United/Divided
Sharp/Dull	Rented/Borrowed
Long/Short	Open/Folded
Slow/Quick	National/Local
Cold/Warm	Ordinary/Exclusive
Old/New	Ascending/Descending
Inner/Outer	Central/Peripheral
Mini/Maxi	Static/Dynamic
Big/Small	Cheap/Expensive
Hollow/Solid	Regular/Irregular
Deep/Shallow	Sophisticated/Vulgar
Single/Double	Original/Conventional
Bottom/Top	Positive/Negative
Closed/Open	Natural/Artificial
Real/Illusory	Interior/Exterior
Frozen/Melted	Theoretical/Practical
Pointed/Blunt	Beginning/Ending

Attributes

Adjustable	Nubby
Ambulating	Odoriferous
Audible	Opposing
Automatic	Organic
Balanced	Portable
Behind	Prolonged
Body-shaped	Protected
Bratty	Quavery
Colorful	Removable
Compressible	Renewable
Disposable	Returnable
Eatable	Rolling
Expandable	Rotating
Extendable	Secured
Fixed	Separable
Flexible	Shining
Floating	Soluble
Fluid	Stationary
Foldable	Streamlined
Formable	Successive
Free	Symbolic
Grouped	Targeted
Hanging	Tawdry
Juxtaposed	Transposed
Leveled	Trivial
Looping	Umpteenth
Manual	Utopian
Mobile	Valorous
Movable	Visual
Nonfat	Wizened

GLOSSARY

Abstract mark A logo or symbol that has no obvious visual relationship to the object it represents; arbitrary mark

Advertising The use of paid media to sell products or communicate ideas

Allusion An indirect reference to a known figure

Arbitrary mark Nonrepresentational mark

Artifact An object made by a person, typically an item of cultural interest

Aspirational positioning Positioning a product or service is a way that people aspire or have ambition to acquire it

Atmospherics Effects intended to create a particular mood, aspects of a brand that may be subconsciously realized

Attitude study An opinion survey to measure changes made in a brand

Audience A specific group at which marketing is aimed

Authenticity The quality of being authentic; *genuineness, legitimacy, truthfulness*

Avatar A brand's icon used across various media

Awareness study A survey measuring an audience's familiarity with a brand

Benefit An advantage or profit gained from a product or service

Brand A person's perception of a product; the strategic personality for a product or company suggesting its values and promises

Brand agency A firm that strategizes, creates, and manages brand building

Brand ambassador A person hired to represent a brand and increase sales

Brand architecture The structure of brands within an organization; the way brands within a company's portfolio are related to and differentiated from one another

Brand asset Any aspect of the brand that has strategic value: attributes, associations, loyalty, etc.

Brand audit Assessment of a brand's strengths and weaknesses

Brand equity The accumulated financial and strategic value of a brand

Brand essence The distillation of a brand's promise into the simplest, shortest possible terms

Brand family A group of related brands and having a "parent" brand that lends authority and trust to the family

Brand gap The distance between brand strategy and customer experience

Brand identity The expression of a brand including its name, trademark, communications, and visual appearance. Brand identity is fundamental to consumer recognition and symbolizes the brand's differentiation from competitors.

Branding The art, science, and practice of building a brand

Brand manager Person responsible for marketing a brand

Brandmark A symbol of a brand, a *trademark*

Brand personality A set of human characteristics that are attributed to a brand name

Brand portfolio The collection of trademarks that a company applies to its products or services

Brand strategy Plan to develop a brand to meet business objectives

Category The arena in which a brand competes

CBO *Chief Brand Officer* Person responsible for coordinating and leading the work of the branding team

Challenger brand Competitor to the leading brand in its category

Charismatic brand A brand that customers feel is essential to their lives

Cliché A trite or overused idea or expression: to be *"avoided like the plague"*

Co-branding When two companies work together to create marketing synergy. Also called *brand partnership*

Co-creation An economic strategy that brings two or more entities together to jointly produce an outcome

Collaboration The process of two or more people or organizations working together to realize or achieve a result

Combination mark A symbol joined with a lettermark or wordmark

Communication The transmission or exchange of information

Concept The basic idea of a mark or advertisement

Concept map A diagram showing connections between ideas

Conceptual noise Competing ideas that obscure clarity

Contrast The degree of difference between light and dark areas. Extreme lights and darks are *high contrast* and medium grays are *low contrast*

Core competencies Essential capabilities that give a company a strategic advantage

Core identity The essential elements of a brand, typically the name and trademark

Core ideology The combination of core purpose and core values

Core purpose Aside from profit, the reason a company exists

Core values The ethics of a company

Corporate identity The brand identity of a company, its *trade dress*

Creative Having imaginative effort; a person paid to produce same

Creative brief A document that sets parameters and defines project goals

Creative strategy An outline including objectives, audience, premise, and theme

Culture jamming Criticizing and subverting advertising and consumerism in the mass media

Customer expectations The anticipated benefits of a brand

Design To plan; to organize with purposeful intent

Design research Examining design processes and the way design affects people

Differentiation The process of defining differences or contrasts among similar products

Display type Letterforms that are intended to be seen first, usually bigger and bolder than *text type*

Disruptive innovation A powerful new idea that creates a new market and disrupts or displaces an existing market

Emotional branding Appealing directly to a consumer's emotional state, needs, and aspirations without rationalization

Ethnography The description of the customs of individual peoples and cultures

Evangelist A zealous brand advocate

Experience design *XD* The practice of designing products, processes, services, events, and environments with the quality of the user's experience foremost

Feature Any aspect of a product or service that distinguishes it from its competitors

Field test A test carried out in the environment in which a product is to be used

Flush A typographic term meaning *visually aligned*

Focus group A research technique in which a small group is led through a discussion about a brand

Font An electronic file containing keystroke-accessible letterforms; wrongly confused with and distinctly different from *typeface*

Generic brand Products distinguished by the absence of a brand name

Global brand A prominent brand with near-universal recognition

Hairline Very thin line, ¼-point or thinner

Icon The visual symbol of a brand; a *trademark*

Information hierarchy Structure and priority given to various pieces of information

Innovation A new idea, device or method, viewed as a better solution that meets unarticulated or existing market needs; something original and more effective

Intellectual property Intangible assets protected by patents and copyrights including names, trademarks, and colors

Italic Types that slant to the right with redrawn letters; often confused with *oblique* types, which are merely roman letterforms angled to the right

Legibility The ability for a design to be read under normal conditions

Letterform The form of a letter of the alphabet, as written or in a typeface.

Lettermark An unpronounceable name formed by letters: CBS, AIGA, TIAA

Leveraging a brand Applying the credibility of one brand to grow another brand; brand extension

Line extension The expansion of a brand family

Logo A readable *wordmark*, commonly misused to mean any trademark

Logotype A combination of parts always shown together, as in a brand's name and symbol

Mark General term referring to any logotype, symbol, emblem, device, insignia, badge, or trademark

Marketing The process of developing, selling, and distributing a product

Market share A brand's percentage of total sales in its category

Master brand An overarching brand name that serves as the main anchoring point on which all underlying and related products are based

Meme An idea or cultural element that is passed from one individual to another

Mental model An explanation of someone's thought process about how something works in the real world

Mission statement A company's (preferably brief) purpose statement

Morpheme A small unit of language that cannot be further divided; used in naming brands

Neologism An invented word that can be legally protected and used as a brand name; found in pharmaceutical branding

Opinion leader Leadership by a person held in high esteem who interprets the meaning of messages or content for lower-end users.

Parallel execution A working methodology in which creative teams develop ideas at the same time

Parent brand A master brand; the cornerstone in a brand family

Perceptual map A diagram of customers' perceptions to understand their behavior

Positioning The brand-building process of differentiating a product to gain a competitive advantage

Posture The angle of stress of a typeface. There are three postures: roman, italic or oblique, and backslant

Product placement Paid advertising in which products or trademarks are put into non-advertising media

Prototype A preliminary model of something that tests an idea; *mockup*

Pure play A company that focuses on a single product or activity instead of various interests

Qualitative research Research on an individual (one-on-one) or small sampling (focus group) scale

Quantitative research Research of a large sampling; polling

Rapid prototyping Techniques used to quickly fabricate a model of a physical part using three-dimensional computer aided design and 3D printing.

Readability The quality of a design to attract and hold a reader's attention

Reputation The opinions of others about an entity; *status, standing, esteem*

Roman An upright, medium-weight typeface

Rule A typeset line

Sans serif Type without cross strokes at the ends of their limbs; *sans* is French for "without"

Segment A group of people who are likely to respond to a message similarly

Segmentation The division of an audience into subgroups with similar values

Signature A person or company's individual mark, assuring authenticity, responsibility, and accountability

Slogan A catchphrase or *tagline*

Social network An affiliation of people who can spread ideas or messages on behalf of a brand

Stakeholder A person with an interest or concern in a business

Store brand A product manufactured especially for a retailer and bearing the retailer's name

Strategy A set of tactics to achieve a business goal

Symbol An icon or trademark that represents a brand

Tactic A specific activity that helps achieve a strategy

Tagline A phrase that summarizes a market position

Target market The group of customers a company has selected to serve

Text type Letterforms that are intended to be seen secondarily, usually smaller and lighter than *display type*

Touchpoint Any point of contact between a buyer and a seller

Trade dress The colors, shapes, typefaces, and design treatments that create a public persona for a company

Trademark A legally protectable name or symbol of a company

Typeface A set of characters that share common characteristics; confused with and distinctly different from *font*

Typo A typographical error, a misspelling

Typography The craft and sometimes art of designing with type; more than mere *typesetting*

U/lc Typesetting using upper and lower case letters

USP *Unique Selling Proposition* An impression that separates a product from its competitors

Value proposition A set of functional and emotional (felt) benefits

Viral marketing The use of memes to cause a branding message to take on a life of its own; the appropriation of social networks for such use

Virtual agency A team of firms that work together to build a brand

Wordmark A trademark that is a readable, pronounceable word; a true logo

Zag A disruptive innovation that runs against prevailing practice; a differentiating idea that drives a brand

INDEX

COLOPHON

The Elements of Logo Design: Design Thinking, Branding, and Making Marks is set in URW Grotesk, a typeface family designed by Hermann Zapf in 1985 for easy, highly legible reading. The type family now has 58 variations of weight, posture, and width. It was designed with a twin serif typeface, URW Antiqua, and the two typefaces share proportions and weights. The two type families were intended for use by a German newspaper publisher, but the project was abandoned and URW subsequently released the typefaces to the public. It came to my attention when I worked briefly with a colleague on a project for URW in the 1990s and "URW Grot" has become one of my most favored types. As a tool, it simply *works*.

The Elements of Logo Design: Design Thinking, Branding, and Making Marks was designed and typeset by the author on a Macintosh using Adobe's InDesign and Photoshop.

CREDITS

My sincere thanks to each art director, designer, and typographer whose work is in this book.

Alex W. White is the author of *The Elements of Graphic Design, Listening to Type: Making Language Visible,* and *Advertising Design and Typography,* among others. His books are used by professionals and at universities all over the world. He is chairman emeritus of the Type Directors Club and is the chair of the graduate program in Design Management at the Shintaro Akatsu School of Design. He lives in Greenwich, Connecticut.
alexanderwwhite.com

"There are books full of logo examples. This book stands out because it discusses graphic design principles and then shows how they apply to logo design. It has fresh insights and different thinking on the process of designing logos. I am delighted to welcome Alex's thoughtful book to my library."
Jerry Kuyper has more than thirty years of experience directing and designing corporate and brand identity programs and has worked for Lippincott, Landor, Siegel & Gale, and Saul Bass & Associates.

jerrykuyper.com